THE MERLINS OF THE
WELSH MARCHES

THE MERLINS OF THE WELSH MARCHES

D.A.ORTON

DAVID & CHARLES
Newton Abbot   London   North Pomfret (Vt)

The author gratefully acknowledges the help given by his wife Margaret who endured wind and weather to supplement his observations. Acknowledgements are due also to H. McSweeney of Aberedw who provided some of the photographs for illustration and vital information on the likely whereabouts of the pairs of merlins which open and close the story.

British Library Cataloguing in Publication Data

Orton, Derek Albert
   The merlins of the Welsh marches.
   1. Merlin (Birds)
   2. Birds – Wales – Borders of Wales
   I. Title
   598.9'1   QL696.F34

   ISBN 0–7153–7992–5

Library of Congress Catalog Card Number
80–66090

Photoset by Northern Phototypesetting Co, Bolton
and printed in Great Britain
by Biddles Ltd, Guildford, Surrey
for David & Charles (Publishers) Limited
Brunel House, Newton Abbot, Devon

Published in the United States of America
by David & Charles Inc
North Pomfret, Vermont 05053, USA

Contents

Foreword

West of the Midland Plain the land rises sharply, its character changing abruptly. Tidy villages, rich arable and lush pasture give way to thorn-studded slopes of steeper gradient, hanging oakwoods, dense conifer plantations. Above the trees are moorlands clothed in nardus grass, bracken, or heather: or a mosaic of all three, interspersed with bilberry. Apart from the valleys of the larger streams and of the rivers, such fields as there are tend to be barren and weed-infested, won grudgingly from the ever-encroaching wilderness. Little beyond the call of curlew and lapwing breaks the silence.

Over the bare hills soar raven and buzzard; the character of the landscape changing in nothing but minor detail from the Brecon Beacons in the south to the Vale of Edeyrnion to the north. The degree of human intrusion varies. The escarpments are riven by steep valleys, each harbouring one or more groups of farm buildings, corrugated iron and breeze-block contrasting none too happily with the weathered grey stone of the dwelling. Cattle graze the brookside meadows; sheep wander in the enclosing slopes. During the summer months, visitors from the towns arrive, but they rarely stray far from the tracks fit for motor vehicles and meadows which are let for caravan parking.

In winter, the high tops are almost devoid of life. Springtime brings the returning migrant birds, their numbers swollen by resident species whose members have wintered on the low-lying land of the valley bottoms. Then the high moors are noisy and active again. Wheatears flash their white rumps; whinchats scold the intruder; meadow pipits flit from one heather spray to another. Such an abundance of potential prey in an open and therefore easily hunted terrain must surely attract predators to harvest the crop?

It does. Sparrowhawks from the wooded valleys below soar up to patrol the tops; the ubiquitous kestrels may be tempted away from their usual diet of voles, mice and beetles. But that is not all.

The pipits, chats and larks returning to their high breeding grounds are sometimes followed by a small, rare and singularly attractive falcon: the merlin. As the well-known kestrel has been refined through the millennia for the capture of small scurrying rodents, so has the merlin specialised in the hunting of small birds in open country – principally the meadow pipit.

The merlin is the smallest of our falcons, perhaps the smallest of our raptors: trim and neat; fast and agile. Usually low-flying and unobtrusive of habit, it may, especially on remote moorland, escape notice. True though this may be, there are now fewer merlins than once there were to attract or escape it. Conifer afforestation of once open heather moor and (since the mid-fifties) the side-effects of cyclodiene pesticides have conspired to thin down populations by as much as 80 per cent.

In 1971, fearing that the figure might soon rise to 100 per cent, I decided that a better acquaintance with the birds might have to be entered into rapidly or not at all. Hence the events on which this book is based.

THE FIRST YEAR

1

The Discovery

The retired keeper was bowed by extreme old age, brown and wrinkled as a withered hazel nut, his accent deeply Welsh. 'The little merlin?' he had queried, digesting the question put to him. 'Yes; several pairs used to nest on the moors. I never shot them. The peregrine, yes. Peregrines without number I have destroyed at the eyrie on the big rocks; but never the little merlin. They do no harm to the grouse, you see . . . and there was a man in London who would always give me a good price for the eggs.' He rambled on, talking of cotton wool, boxes marked 'fragile' and candle-grease dripped into blown egg-shells.

Now, we were on our way up the rough track indicated on the map, enjoying the refreshment of the cool breeze found at 800ft on a bright morning in early May. Heat haze had yet to form: distant ridges stood sharply defined, each with its hovering kestrel or soaring buzzard. Larks climbed high in the crisp air, pouring down silver showers of song. Any heather clump standing proud of its fellows bore twittering meadow pipit or clacking wheatear.

Curlews called, lapwings displayed overhead, diving to screech protest at the intrusion. To the left of the track a valley opened towards the west. Ancient hawthorns grew on the gentle slopes flanking it, harbouring whitethroat, chaffinch, blackbird and ring ousel, all singing. Our track climbed higher. 'Look for tall heather above the 1,000ft contour,' had been the message. That altitude had now been reached and the heather grew tall, evidently unburned for many years.

Reflections on the possibilities were interrupted suddenly by a ringing chatter from close at hand. A moment later, a small slate-blue raptor burst from the heather on our right, rising rocket-like on fast-beating wings to circle over whatever lay beyond. Soon, it was high overhead, but side-slipping from view. Progress through the heather, made with the aim of keeping the bird in view as long as possible, was brought up short by the discovery that it had risen from a perch on the rim of a concealed line of low cliffs surrounding a singularly secluded natural amphitheatre.

The merlin continued to circle, gaining both speed and height and calling harshly with scarce a break. Beyond the amphitheatre the land fell steeply to the farmlands below. Beyond these, sunlight glinted on the waves of a distant reservoir; after that, blue haze. For more than five minutes binoculars had been held on a high fast-moving bird. 12×60s, they weighed 3½lb. Regret was not wholly unmingled with relief when, quite abruptly, he began to plane down, then fell in a fast but shallow stoop to alight in the crown of a ragged hawthorn on the far side of the amphitheatre. From that, via another, he soon retreated, to vanish in the heather on the moor beyond the farthest rocks.

The constant companion of my wilderness birdwatching, who has certainly learned the full implications of the phrase 'for better or for worse', expressed her pleasure at what we had at last been privileged to see. The object of rapt attention gone from the scene, the exceptional beauty of the prospect was able to make its full impact on the eye. The cliff wall was in the shape of a horse-shoe; the floor of the amphitheatre enclosed, broad and comparatively level, but nevertheless the source of a tiny stream which sprang from among a clump of hawthorns then barely in leaf. Other thorns were dotted here and there, some isolated, others in small clumps. One, which happened to be the largest, contained the disused nest of a carrion crow. The sward was of grass, cropped short by sheep, interspersed with bilberry, called locally by the name 'whinberry', and bracken which extended up the slopes to where they terminated in the vertical rock of the cliff wall.

A buzzard floated up from the farmland below, approached nearer and made to cross the amphitheatre. Suddenly, like a jack-in-the-box, the merlin was airborne again, ringing up to gain the height-gauge of his so-far unconscious victim. Down he came, pouring out his fierce chatter of rage. This did not look like mere demonstration, and the stooping falcon appeared to have taken for his point of aim the big hawk's spine between the wing-roots. Narrowly, by intention or otherwise, the merlin missed his target, which shifted ponderously, mewing in protest. Then, the staccato chatter of the cock was supplemented by the raucously drawn out screams of his mate as she rose to lend her support. On this occasion, it proved to be of the moral order only, but was enough to expedite the departure of the intruder which quit the scene of the encounter with broad sails beating rather more energetically than usual.

After their victory, the merlin pair celebrated with a display flight which took them high over the area. Watching them closely, it was noted that the generally brown effect of the plumage of the hen, contrasting with the slatey hues of the cock, were each distinguishable through binoculars, in good light, at ranges exceeding half a mile.

So there was a pair. That, on 2 May, must surely mean an intention to breed somewhere not so very far away. Indeed, the vigorous defence made against the encroaching buzzard implied the probability that we stood on or by the exact site the birds had earmarked for their own. Both merlins concluded the display by dropping into the heather just the other side of the head of a deep valley beyond the amphitheatre. Perhaps we should stroll over and see what, if anything, was to be seen there? Curiosity conflicted with a concern to obey strictly the law protecting this rare falcon from disturbance. Nor was that the only consideration. Whatever the law might or might not allow, we did not wish to distress the birds. We would try moving a little nearer, but would be governed by their reactions. If they were content with nothing less than total retreat, then so be it. Merlin welfare must precede and override curiosity about merlins.

Making our way along the valley rim, we found pile after pile of pipit feathers – all from comparatively recent kills – confirming our view that we were in the proposed nesting territory. Books speak of a 'plucking post' in its vicinity, suggesting that a single stump or rock is automatically selected. That is not always the case. Sometimes, 'plucking area' would be a better term. The merlins had littered every rock, stump, anthill and tussock for fifty yards with feathers. Every pile of feathers but one originated from a meadow pipit. The exception was a collection of brighter brown feathers from a skylark.

The track led towards and past the head of the valley. Another track branched off to the right. As it went in the desired direction, we took it. From the head of the valley, when we reached it, a deep ravine beyond came into view. The banks were clad in deep heather, unburned for many years. Out of it came the cock merlin, to fly rapidly up the ravine, silently after one short burst of yikking, and out of sight in a fold of the ground.

The bird's relative silence on departure provoked thought: had we found the precise site of the nest? If so, hard luck. The lie of the land would not allow us to watch it from a distance sufficient to rule out the risk of disturbance. A little disappointed, we withdrew for lunch. On the way back to the car, we put the merlin up again from exactly where he had been perched at the time of the first encounter. Again he rose clamorously to circle the valley, but on this occasion his mate did not join him.

2
The Afternoon

Back at the car, lunch was not altogether uneventful. A pair of wheatears took turns to observe us closely from a handy gatepost: ravens played, croaked and cackled in the sky overhead. As we kept the moorland heights under periodic scrutiny, a small hawk, thought to be the cock merlin, was seen to fall in an impressive vertical stoop from high above the heat haze in which the skyline now shimmered. From a stand of larches 300yd away a hen sparrowhawk ringed up to where she was but a speck in the blue. Watching her, I picked up a still more distant bird, so high that even 12×60 binoculars could not establish with certainty whether it was merely another buzzard or a kite far to the south-east of their usual summer range. Wing and tail profiles were distorted by the haze, but sunlight reflected from a head significantly pale in hue.

Lunch concluded, we climbed back up the hill-track, laboriously in the afternoon heat. As we had put up the merlin from two different places which might have been nest-sites, we decided to watch from a vantage point covering both, 200yd from one, 400yd from the other. It would not, we thought, yield a view enabling us to pinpoint the actual nest, which was not in any case a prime intention; but it might afford us more good views of merlins in flight, which was. It did; although heat haze now blurred the sharp definitions of the cool morning. Seated comfortably among heather clumps, back-rests provided by convenient rocks, we searched the pinnacles and buttresses farther along the cliffs. 'There's something on a rock just past where that little twisted thorn juts from the cliff face,' murmured my companion. 'It may only be a pigeon. But it's blue, for certain.' As she spoke, my more powerful binoculars found the bird. As I adjusted focus, it took off, flew along the cliffs to another ledge, paused briefly, then rose skywards as though jet-propelled by the bursts of harsh sound it again uttered as it climbed.

Some pigeon! The hen came out of the ravine at similar speed to join her mate in a display of aerobatics which lasted for nearly a quarter of an hour. Higher and higher they flew, up among the darting swallows to where haze and distance together turned all birds into shimmering blobs or specks. Eventually, the 'merlin' I was by then intent upon circled near enough to be recognised for the swallow it was, busily hunting midges high over the valley. An urgent sweep of the entire sky discovered the hen merlin – the authentic hen merlin – diving towards the ravine, the cock close on her tail. So the ravine it was. Or was it? Observation continued patiently, hopes of clarification that day still very much alive.

Another buzzard soared in, to pass directly over the ravine. Up went the steel-blue interceptor, to repeat the morning's performance. Away, in short order, went the buzzard. The merlin dropped back to the ravine. Kestrels, several different kestrels, had from time to time approached the far side of the ravine unchallenged. Now, one came to hover directly above where I was beginning to suppose the merlins' nest was or would shortly be. This should be interesting; perhaps conclusive. Up rocketed the cock merlin, swiftly but in unexpected silence. Rising to the exact altitude of the hovering kestrel, he side-slipped towards it, hovered momentarily wing-tip to wing-tip, banked round in a tight circle . . . then side-slipped away without so much as a yik of protest. The kestrel, an adult male, hovered on unconcerned.

My glasses were lowered in astonishment. Why such hostility to a buzzard? Why this fraternal tolerance of a kestrel? Although neither competed seriously with the bird-hunting merlin for prey, the kestrel surely approached nearer to competitor status than the bigger hawk, which lacked the agility as well as the inclination to hunt pipits with much hope of success. Nor did either represent any direct threat. Or did it? Both buzzard and kestrel were principally hunters of ground-game; in the former case anything from a leveret to a beetle;

similarly in the latter, but excluding items larger than an infant rabbit. In both cases, the chicks or nestlings of ground-nesting birds might be taken. Why, therefore, should the sometime ground-nesting merlin tolerate either bird prospecting or hunting over its territory? An interesting question to which a plausible answer was not slow to present itself.

Kestrels, too, may nest in the heather. Their down-covered nestlings differ but little from those of the merlin while either are still small enough to be under threat. Perhaps the inhibition which protected such nestlings from the hunting-fervour of their parents extended fortuitously to cover also the nestlings of closely related species? An inhibition to which the buzzard, as a far larger bird and a tree-nester to boot, was not subject? This the merlin would not 'know' as you or I might know it, but the processes of natural selection, working through the many millennia during which these birds have shared moorland habitats, might well have refined a position in which merlins sharply hostile to buzzards had tended more often to rear their young, while hostility to kestrels was merely an irrelevance. The one attribute would therefore become stamped upon the behaviour pattern of the species; the other would continue spasmodically or not at all. Perhaps this theory, like the location of the nest site, would be confirmed or denied by further observations.

Our day was concluded by the cock merlin making what appeared to be a hunting flight, although no pursuit or capture was witnessed. He rose slowly in widening circles, ascending to a height no more than 20ft above the heather, his flight fast, his wing-beat shallow. Shallow-angle stoops were made at each and every patch of cover capable of sheltering a pipit. But none was flushed. A faint depression offered him a scrap of dead ground for his eventual disappearance. It was not disdained. The name 'merlin' derives supposedly from the French *émerillon*; having no connection, it is claimed, with 'Merlin' as a symbol of magical power. The extraordinary capacity of the bird to de-materialise itself (so far as the watching human eye is concerned) in a fold of ground only inches below the general lie of the land, leads to doubts on this point. Of all birds I have watched, the merlin alone – magical derivation or not – possesses this ability to draw about itself such a cloak of virtual invisibility.

3

The First Year Progresses

Having at last run to earth a pair of merlins with an evident intention to breed, bird-watching and other plans were naturally centred upon them. But, as the poet said so truly, 'The best laid schemes o' mice an' men gang aft a-gley.'

In mid-May, a telephone call to a local contact established that for a fortnight no fresh kills had been found near the presumed site, but no further opportunity for a visit came until 4 June. Rain-bedraggled remnants of old kills littered the rim of the rocks, but not a trace of a newly killed bird of any species. Nor was a merlin seen or heard during a three-hour vigil. We walked across the moor to what was thought to be the most favoured hunting range. Alive with pipits it certainly was; and the weather good for flying. Buzzards and kestrels were aloft; a hen sparrowhawk from the oakwoods below came up to the moor, caught a young pipit and ate it from her foot as she flew: but no merlin. The nearest thing to one, a 'possible' on the haze-distorted skyline, recorded as a 'merlin-like UFO'.

The hills cover an area between one and two miles in width, but extend in length for four times that distance. They are bounded by other ranges which to the human eye look equally good or even better merlin terrain. But for some reason known only to themselves, merlins eschew the surrounding hills, concentrating – in the days when there were enough merlins for the word to have meaning – in this comparatively restricted area. Before 1950, anything from two to five pairs might be found nesting there. But in years when there were but two pairs, a site at either end of the hills would be chosen in preference to others more centrally situated. Obviously, therefore, the opposite end of the feature was the next place to investigate; especially so as merlins which had gone through the full routine of territorial defence at one end of the hills had been known before to decamp inexplicably to nest at the other.

So there we went: to make a steeper and appreciably more exacting climb in weather now uncomfortably warmer. There, the track runs between long ridges from near one end of which a broad dingle opens and sweeps down to the fertile valley below. Towards its head, the banks are steep and heather-covered. Here, traditionally, was the most regularly occupied merlin site in the entire area. What is more, its position and the lie of the land are such that it may be kept under observation with high-power glasses from a distance at which there is no conflict between effective observation and the avoidance of disturbance. It did not prove difficult to find.

Oak and ash grew in the dingle, but fewer thorns. Wood and willow warblers were there; ring ousels 'tuk-tukked' among the rocks above the swiftly flowing stream. Pipits were fewer, but many whinchats called from the bracken. There was without doubt a supply of prey sufficient to rear a family of merlins. A morning's observation, however, yielded nothing. That, on 13 June, looked rather like conclusive evidence. It is usual for merlins in Wales to lay early in May, and hatch in early June. By the 13th, hunting should have been intensive, ensuring a sighting. But, after all, birds are not automata, nor could the possibility of a stolen first clutch and a repeat be ruled out.

The discussion which followed led to a withdrawal higher up the track. To its highest point, in fact, where both enclosing ridges and the far end of the valley came into view. We sat back to back (no convenient slopes and arm-chair rocks here!) to begin our second vigil.

Immediately I spotted a bird taken to be a sparrowhawk flying in characteristic fashion. A few wing-beats were followed by a slow well-banked glide as it prospected the heather with the formidable thoroughness typical of the species. No small bird visible from any angle above was likely to be missed; nothing was scamped, nothing neglected. The terrain was worked methodically, as a good gun-dog would work it. There seemed little purpose to be served by using the binoculars, but I raised them just the same. Through them, the 'sparrowhawk' was seen to have the long pointed wings of a hen merlin. Something else had been learned. Merlins may prospect for prey using exactly the same technique as the sparrowhawk, a bird associated conventionally with very different habitat. There was more to the merlin, then, than mere dash and impetuosity. Still hunting methodically and with meticulous care, she passed close by, evidently unconcerned by our presence. We saw how the pale rufous sides to her neck almost united to form a collar; how faint were her moustachial stripes. The impression given by her heavily streaked breast was more one of mottling; and her tail, not so very much shorter than a kestrel's, appeared to have been 'reverse printed'. In other words, the dark bars occupied more space than the paler ground colour. Flying slowly with leisured beat, she was no less elegant than her graceful cousin.

She flew on to work her way up the bracken slope to our left and vanish over the crest without flushing or finding prey. The hen, hunting on the afternoon of 13 June: what might be the implication of that? We could but guess, confirmed in our suspicions that there had been a failure to breed. Twenty minutes after her departure, her mate came speeding along the ridge over which she had vanished to stoop over my head like a blue shooting star and vanish into dead ground beyond the heather at the head of the dingle in which the traditional site was situated. Of one thing I was certain. There had been nothing in his talons when he passed overhead. What should we now conclude? What; if anything, should we do? Wait and see.

The following two hours produced kestrel, buzzard, black-headed gull, an unexpected redshank, an even more unexpected teal, but no more merlin sightings. As evening drew on, empty stomachs dictated a decision to retire. We strolled slowly back along the track, keeping a weather eye on the ridges. Whinchats scolded from the bracken. The few seams in the hillside capable of harbouring a tree or bush were each occupied by a pair of blackbirds or ring ousels, the former having in recent years colonised the high moors once left to their less common relatives.

Suddenly, a silhouette becoming ever more familiar flashed above the skyline, wings flickering in a blur. Gone again. Was it to be just that one glimpse, or more? More: gloriously more. The cock merlin, for he it was, shot vertically up over the skyline, wings closed in the classical posture of the stooping falcon, the laws of gravity set impudently at defiance. Rolling slowly over at the apex of his zoom, he opened his wings, beat down almost vertically with astonishing velocity, brushed a heather spray, shot upwards again with wings all but closed, and appeared to eat an insect from his talons as he again rolled over at the zenith of his ascent. Then, instead of diving back below the ridge, he passed at high speed directly overhead and down the big dingle where the old nest site had been.

The evening sun shone through a gap in the thunderclouds piling up on the horizon behind us. Its rays caught the merlin as he passed over, inflaming his breast to vivid gold. As he banked to streak down the dingle, wings and tail flashed blue as sapphire. Surely the bird of 2 May again. Could there be two of such brilliant hue? But where had he gone now? He reappeared; flying swiftly along the ridge from behind which he had first shown. A bird climbed to meet him. His mate. Joyfully, they filled the sky with their play; play quite different from that which had taken place over the other valley in May. Now, the birds did much more than circle together. They strived, so it seemed, to excel each other's speed, agility and noise. They reciprocated the most subtle and sophisticated of aerial ploys; climbing vertically, beating back to within inches of the ground, accelerating as they approached it, to wrench themselves away from it in a flash, generating forces which might be thought sufficient to tear a small bird apart. They stooped at each other, supple tails fanning rapidly open and closed, flexing to turn the birds in jinks and twists too fast for the human eye to follow in detail. Lightning approaches were evaded by an inch or less in some manoeuvre which would simultaneously position the escaping bird to launch a counter-attack of equal mock-ferocity. For half an hour, this brilliant display continued. The energy of the birds seemed inexhaustible. Not so ours. Breathless, numb of arm, eyes growing strained and sore, we wilted. Still flying with undiminished *élan*, the merlins moved up-valley into the setting sun now almost lost behind the high-piled nimbus cloud. Brown or blue falcons no more: just darker silhouettes against a background of looming grey sky. We left them to their unexplained jubilation; ourselves prey to more mundane considerations.

4

The Conclusion of the First Year

Tradition has it that merlins in flight hug the ground. So they often do. We left the valley a little stunned by what they were capable of high in the sky when the spirit moved them, but still uncertain as to whether they had bred. Their behaviour, although thrilling to watch, had seemed rather too much like an out of season courtship display. On balance, we formed the opinion that this pair had not nested successfully. But why not? Perhaps they were infertile from pesticide residues. Perhaps there had been too much human disturbance, our own included.

For the remainder of June and in early July other commitments frustrated our desire to be in the hills with the merlins. On 11 July an opportunity was seized but yielded nothing of note.

17 July was spent investigating another range of hills a few miles to the north; then came 18 July. Acting again on 'information received' we took a different route across the moor, one which brought us to an undulating plateau of heather about mid-way between the two sites where merlins had been found. Looking in one direction, the misty outlines of the hills bordering the second valley could just be made out; in the opposite direction, the vista was closed by a ridge no more than half a mile away. The moor rose gently towards it, the heather healthy, thick and tall. To the west, there was a small depression in the ground. Muddy, overgrown with marsh plants, it was half filled with water. From it, a tiny streamlet trickled away between steep banks crowned with heather clumps. Beyond, the moor climbed to another low ridge.

A pair of carrion crows paddled in the margins. Woodpigeons flew in to drink, but did not remain. A party of black-headed gulls indicated by their behaviour a conviction of proprietorship. A snipe strutted in circles, its long bill probe-probe-probing the mud. A shape tinted rufous flashed by my ear: a heather-hopping kestrel so intent upon its hunting that it had failed to notice us sitting there. A meadow pipit fled before it, evidently convinced that it was the object of the hawk's attentions. The kestrel swung away, soared briefly, then settled down to a steady job of hovering.

A quarter of an hour passed, without the binoculars registering anything of special interest. I lowered them. Suddenly, over the little pool, a gull was in pursuit of a smaller, darker, bird. Up with the glasses again. A long-winged raptor, but dull slate in the cloud-obscured light. The merlin? I dithered. Caught by some trick of distance and perspective, the bird seemed too large. And certainly not blue enough. A peregrine tiercel, perhaps. This was, after all, a recognised peregrine territory before the population collapse in the mid fifties. Highly improbable. Measure the fugitive against the size of the pursuing gull. And what of the black bandit-mask of the larger falcon? Not a trace of it. Undoubtedly the merlin, looking dull and washed out in the ungenerous light.

He flew round the pool in circles of increasing radius, the gull hot in pursuit. Suddenly the latter became aware of the fact that it had been led well away from the protection of its clamorously croaking companions. Breaking off abruptly, it flew back to them, aggressive no longer. The merlin allowed matters to rest at that and settled on the embankment of the little stream to preen. The sun at last broke through, dispersing the dense pall of cloud and illuminating the merlin so that we recognised him without further doubt as our discovery of May and June.

After ten minutes more, he flew to another heather clump, making a half-hearted pass at the snipe *en route*. The snipe retreated into the reeds: the merlin settled to preen those parts of his plumage which had so far escaped attention.

Fifteen minutes later, he took off, encouraged perhaps by a light breeze which had risen, to beat to and fro along the ridge beyond the pool. Gaining height, at first with some labour, he rose faster as he reached the drier air above and began to soar on wide-stretched motionless wings. Two sheep ambled across the skyline towards us. The merlin stooped swiftly at the leader, pulling away vertically a foot from its woolly back. The sheep plodded on, unaware of the service it had performed in helping the bird dispel aggression generated by the interfering gull. The velocity of the stoop carried the merlin back into the higher air, where it climbed rapidly. Two stock doves approached, flying 50ft above it. With an explosion of energy, the merlin shot up to attack. The assault was determined and may well have been in earnest, lethal intent implied by the bird's every movement. Already travelling fast, the doves accelerated sharply; the bird under attack jinking and side-slipping. For fifteen seconds or more the merlin flashed and twisted in hot pursuit; then, unaccountably, as though suddenly bored by the affair, turned away. The attack broken off, the doves sped no less urgently for the horizon, two fast-diminishing dots in the binoculars.

Higher and higher soared the merlin, now serene and relaxed, riding the air currents in a sky now blue, flecked with snow-white cloud. Up there, heat haze had but minimal effect as we gazed through glasses held nearly vertical at the small falcon soaring 2,000ft above our heads. Sharp and clear his outline as he slowly drew in wings to fall in a shallow gently accelerating stoop towards the valley graced by his brilliant aerobatics on that memorable evening of the previous month.

To try and regain contact with the bird was a temptation beyond resisting. We walked sharply back to the car, drove down the near-unmotorable track, then through narrow single-track lanes to a farmhouse which marked the limits of human occupation. Leaving the car there, we climbed a steep lane which petered out into another rough track leading up by a rushing stream. Trees lined the steep banks, growing progressively more stunted as we climbed. Cattle gave way to sheep, the pastures stonier and more neglected. Songbirds thinned out, lapwings began to scream overhead.

We climbed farther. Stone dykes gave way to post and wire fences; then to no fences at all. Heather clumps appeared among the sheep-grazed turf. To the left of the track, bracken; forming a clean line which divided the cultivated from the wild. We climbed for an hour, in growing heat. What an inordinate amount of trouble to take to catch up with a merlin which might by now have circled back to perch by the little pool, dozing and preening by turns, oblivious of the interest inspired. The site of the June adventure lay another half-hour's walk ahead. The sun glared down. Time to halt for coffee and a sandwich. Put the heavy binoculars away while we refreshed ourselves? Not likely. One never knew what might turn up. 'Oh!' cried my wife, 'look at that family of kestrels playing in the sky over the ridge.' Up with the binoculars. Three brown merlins made playful and elegant passes at each other. Gradually, they circled nearer. Two looked identical, one slightly different. Mum and the kids? There seemed little or no reasonable doubt. But whose kids? Was there an authentic breeding pair present *in addition to* the merlins we had been sporadically watching? Or had we been 'sold the dummy' regarding almost everything? It seemed not unlikely.

The three birds, still in lively play, worked their way back to the ridge from beyond which they had appeared and passed from view. We sat and reflected. Half an hour went by. We stood up and packed the rucksack. From the ridge came a merlin, flying straight and fast, directly overhead, 50ft up: the hen. 10ft higher and 5yd to her rear flew her mate, his breast shining orange in the sunlight. As he passed overhead and away, the angle of view changed. His tail, shoulders and the upper surfaces of his wings caught the light. Blue, brilliant blue. Either there were two surprisingly colourful cock merlins on these hills, or our hero was the father of the family at last discovered. All too soon, autumn was at hand; and with it the exodus of the merlins from the high moors. It now remained only to speculate on what 1972 might have in store.

THE SECOND YEAR

5
1972 Opens

The arrival of April 1972 had been awaited with impatience. The 23rd of the month found us back on the merlin moors, implementing plans made in the previous autumn. With action in 1971 at both extremities of the feature, the key question for 1972 had been where to concentrate. Again, local information came to our aid. A few minutes' walk from the little pool in the heather where the cock merlin had dissipated his aggressions on sheep and attacked the stock dove, there was a stand of oaks and sycamores. It was an empty rectangle, planted many years ago to shelter a *hafod* or summer dwelling, long obliterated by the ravages of time and weather.

Here, traditionally, the merlins performed their mating ceremonies; including a celebrated wild pursuit round and round the trees. This section of the moor, therefore, seemed to be the likeliest place to open the season, despite the events of the previous May and July, and where they had taken place. But the site of past adventure holds a magnetic attraction. Setting painstakingly obtained local advice at nought, we chose to inspect first the long valley where in July we had at last seen the whole merlin family. Our approach was via the steep track at the far end. Despite cold, dull, weather the birds were active. Over the pyramid-shaped hill by which the car was left, a mixed party of eight ravens, four crows and a single buzzard sampled the air currents in peaceful coexistence.

The track was still flooded with the remains of winter's rains; tadpoles by the hundred wriggled in the larger puddles. Snipe were flushed; we heard our first cuckoo of the year. Higher and higher we climbed, until the crest was reached.

Two hours passed, the weather slowly improving. Kestrel, raven, buzzard and black-headed gull put in appearances; pipits there were in plenty, but fewer whinchats. No ring ousel sang or flew. As the minutes ticked by, so the information regarding the courtship oaks reasserted a grip on our imaginations. We grew restless. Footsteps could be retraced to the car, a circuitous route could be driven and the hills re-entered from another direction. Were that done, we should be twenty minutes' walk from our objective. Alternatively, we could walk on directly across the hills, covering somewhat less ground than we had already traversed to end up in the same place, new terrain having been investigated *en route*. That was the decision we finally reached.

The new terrain yielded little but fresh views of distant hills and a pair of redshank apparently tadpole-hunting in an exceptionally large puddle. After the redshank, grouse. Unremarkable on those hills, but a welcome sight as they perched on small eminences to chide us. 'Go back – go back – go back,' they called, proud red wattles aflame with territorial indignation.

A little leg-weary, we reached our destination. A pair of ring ousels displayed in a nearby blackthorn, but no merlins pursued each other round the oaks and sycamores. That we should have found them so engaged on our arrival was, of course, far too much to have reasonably hoped for. Bracken stretched as far as the eye could see: whinchats flitted and scolded. Hunting terrain for merlins, no doubt, but a dearth of heather or thorn trees bearing crows' nests; even of the sort of perches fancied by them. As we had crossed the hills, there had been one sign of the merlins' presence: a pile of freshly plucked skylark feathers. Sparrowhawks, too, may kill skylarks, but the feathers had been found at an altitude where sparrowhawks might not hunt so early in the year. So there were grounds for persistence.

The tradition of the courtship flights notwithstanding, the terrain, virtually devoid of heather, did not look right. Merlins, I knew, nested occasionally in other ground vegetation, but not when good heather might be found somewhere in the vicinity. It seemed that we might as well plod on to the small pool. There, at least, heather grew abundantly. Eventually, we approached the skyline from which it would come into view. There it was; but no longer small, after the winter rains. Gulls galore were there in raucous residence; skylines shimmered again in a heat-haze, whatever the sensitive human epidermis might register.

A bird took off from the heather four or five hundred yards away, observed purely by the chance of where the glasses happened to be directed at the time. A cock merlin, brightly coloured. After flying 200yd across our front, he alighted. We moved forward, using dead ground as carefully as might the merlin himself. Our reward was ten minutes with the bird in view from a halved distance. Bluish back; bright gold underparts. Our friend of 1971 appeared to have survived the winter in good order. Could we, perhaps, get closer still? We tried, but the merlin had had enough. He was off in a flash, flying fast and low, directly away from us. Banking, he entered a fold in the ground and was not seen to emerge. Our route back to the track gave us a view into it, but he was not there. The track now ran level for some way, so the labour of continuing to follow it was slight. We were so far from the car that another half-mile was neither here nor there. 'Look over there,' called the third member of the party, a sharp-eyed young man in his teens, on the moor for the first time.

There, quite high in the sky, slightly distorted by haze, circled three birds. Two were merlins, the third a kestrel which had joined them in their display-flight evidently unresented. The merlin display was a muted version of what we had seen the previous May. Move by move, the kestrel reciprocated it. 'So you think merlins fly nicely?' he seemed to say. 'Just watch me then. . . . And I'm not even trying!' The merlin display livened into sprightly attack and evasion. Eventually, the hen dived away out of sight beyond the edge of the escarpment, her mate close behind. The hen kestrel floated up to join the cock, a pattern of circling and counter-circling following.

Gradually, the kestrels drifted away to find a ridge to hover above side by side. For us to continue farther involved another climb. We sat and relaxed weary leg muscles. Let the mountain come to Mahomet. It didn't.

The walk back was comparatively uneventful, until we reached a bend in the track only half an hour's walk from the car. A pile of cock blackbird feathers fluttered in the breeze. Fresh feathers; some stained with uncongealed blood. Had the merlins back-tracked us? Or were there two pairs on the hills this year? Or had we found the handiwork of some marauding sparrowhawk, come up to hunt from the wooded country below, in pursuit, perhaps, of a blackbird flushed from cover below and manouevred cunningly to where it would find no other? Questions are one thing: answers another.

6
The Breakthrough

30 April was spent on the moor, in what were to be endeavours to improve our acquaintance with the merlins. Not so much as a hint of one; not even a fresh kill. Depression began to set in. Were they just a pair in passage, on their way farther north? Perhaps that was all we had seen in 1971. A pair on their way north in May, a family party on its way south in July. That, of course, was merely disappointment talking. As a hypothesis, it was supported by only a selection of the facts.

The next visit, made on 6 May, began uneventfully. The party, a little larger than usual, explored the moor in a now familiar pattern, the return-march taking us via the pool. The usual snipe had not flown as we approached it and I found his feathers littered on an ant-hill, his comical bill and indigestible feet lying at the foot of it. A sad sight; but indicative that the merlins still occupied the moor. Taking care not to draw attention to my grisly discovery, I gestured to signal the way back to the car, which lay along the course of the streamlet. We entered the defile one by one, myself bringing up the rear. Suddenly, that critical spot between the shoulder-blades tingled with extra-sensory perception: eyes, for sure, were upon me. Round I whipped; glasses at the ready, to find a bird quartering the moor 500yd away. The glasses, as I expected them to, established it to be a merlin. The hunter grows attuned to his quarry.

In that light, a merlin of nondescript colour, but beyond doubt a merlin. We all had a good view of it, so my friends had not journeyed in vain after all. The bird hunted methodically, often turning into the breeze as though on the point of hovering like a kestrel. But always, as mouths opened to comment on the fact, it would side-slip off pitch after just two or three wing-strokes. Flying an erratic course, it gradually worked away from us. As usual, the performance was concluded by the bird entering a fold in the ground from which it was not seen to emerge.

It had not escaped me that the merlin's course, if continued, would take it to that part of the moors where we had first made their acquaintance. Somewhere we had not so far checked this year. I made the obvious proposal, which received assent. The walk, uphill and down-dale, took an hour and a half, during which time the weather showed signs of a belated improvement. As the sky lifted, birds grew more active; pipits, chats and wheatears materialising as though from thin air to observe our progress from heather clump and bracken spray. At last, we reached the gorge and the head of the valley. No merlin rose chattering, which slightly damped risen hopes. So it became a matter of examining the valley bush by bush, tree by tree, rock by rock. First, perhaps, to catch a glimpse of fast-departing merlin, then for tell-tale heaps of fresh pipit feathers.

The amphitheatre itself may be entered from that direction by one of several steep-sided clefts in the rocks. Boulder and pebble-strewn as they are, it is not easy to pick a way down them in unbroken silence. This, however, we contrived to do. Alerted by an opportune flash of instinct, I ensured that the last few yards were covered with Red Indian stealth. We took up a position from which most of the upper valley was in view, but from which nothing would be visible to keen eyes peering therefrom but tweed hats, tips of noses and lenses of binoculars. Merlins, unless they have suffered persecution, bear themselves boldly in the presence of Earth's most dreaded predator. Unless the sun's rays gleamed capriciously to reflect from binocular lenses, we might hope to get a good enough look at any merlin perched there in view before it decided on departure.

That, as it transpired, proved to be the understatement of the year. A number of thorns, some comparatively robust, others in part withered, grew at intervals from the face of the rock which formed much of the enclosing wall. The nearest thrust out its abbreviated trunk horizontally, about 50yd from where we stood. On it, preening and facing away from us, sat a merlin. A merlin too grey to be recognised readily as a hen; but certainly not blue enough to be the cock we had come to know. The bird turned on its perch, still unaware of us. Breast and belly were paler and less heavily marked than earlier sightings had led me to expect. The bird was restless, and turned again. As it presented its back for a second scrutiny, the sun broke through, warming the colour from grey to washed-out sepia. Not a radical transformation, perhaps, but sufficient to clarify the issue. This bird was a hen; possibly deficient in pigmentation; or perhaps an older – or younger? – bird than others so far encountered.

Cramped by ten minutes of motionless observation, someone drew breath audibly, sought to ease his position soundlessly. He failed, having sent a small pebble tinkling down the rocks. In a flurry of fast-flailing wings, the merlin was away; rising fast, heading in the direction from which it and we had come.

We moved out into the valley bottom to find less discomfort by sitting on hummocks in the turf behind a patch of dead bracken. Immediately, a young cock sparrowhawk floated into view, following the line of the farther rim of the valley. Kicked into violent action by the sight of prey, the hawk tilted over and shot away like a bullet. A lapwing chick reappeared from beneath its motionless mother to resume exploration at the foot of the big hawthorn wherein the crows had built their nest, now obscured by dense green foliage.

The stage began to fill. Woodpigeons; a pair of curlews; the other parent lapwing. Then a pair of ring ousels hopped into view and began to dig for worms. Handsome specimens both, the hen bearing a gorget-crescent hardly less bold than that of her mate. The ousels, seeing something which had escaped the human eye, fled quietly to cover. The sharp, slightly gutteral cry of the cock merlin rang out. A second bird called. The merlin pair was present, although invisible. But did this presence imply an intention to nest? We were as far from firm information on this point as ever.

Time had come for departure, unless we fancied going dinner-less to bed. The long plod back to the car was uneventful; unless one counts a pony removing the caul from a new-born foal and a fox-kill so fresh that the viscera squeezed from the unfortunate grouse were still warm and steaming.

The events of the 6th had decided how the week-end of the 13th/14th was to be employed: the amphitheatre and the adjacent gorge must have exclusive attention. Since the wind had remained in the same quarter all the week, we sought the same sheltered spot from which we had previously watched. After an hour of inactivity in which the weather, threatening on arrival, showed promise of improvement, I experienced an impulse to inspect for remnants of kills and pellets the bush growing from the valley wall where the hen merlin had preened in full view. Merlins, like other birds of prey, cast up, after they have fed, an oval pellet consisting of the feathers, larger bones which may have been swallowed, and other indigestible debris from their prey. Some scrambling was entailed, but soon I sat by where the merlin had perched, finding pipit feathers in large numbers, a merlin's moulted tail feather (which I have in my possession still) and four pellets.

So the use of this particular perch last Saturday had not been wholly a matter of chance. As though to underline this conclusion, a merlin broke from cover to circle the valley 'yik-yik-yikking' with frantic excitement. Round and round it flew; wings beaten into a blur broken by short banked glides but with never a break in the din of protest. Protest at my occupation of a plucking post, or something more? The ludicrously obvious conclusion still evaded me. The lapwing pair took off in pursuit, mobbing hard and provoking vigorous retaliation. Vigorous retaliation, but no evident attempt at a lethal response. After perching briefly in several different hawthorns, her perchings serving to punctuate her flights, the hen merlin (for she it was) vanished over the rim of the rocks, still calling. I strolled back to my observation post, still impervious to what was going on. It required a second flight by the hen merlin and a gloriously savage attack by the cock on an intruding buzzard right overhead to clear the blockage and allow the penny to drop. At last, the significance of the crows' old nest in the hawthorn was apparent. So much for the local opinion which insisted that merlins in those parts were all heather-nesters.

Within five minutes of my return to our semi-concealed OP, both merlins came back, each from a different direction, to arrive at the tree together. The cock went straight in to brood; the hen flew on to alight on a rock nearer to us than to the nest. This we noted with relief and pleasure. It seemed a reasonable indication that the effects of the disturbance had not been profound. Further confirmation of this was given when she settled down to perform a long and methodical preen, a procedure arguing relaxation and self-assurance. Half an hour later, the cock called 'eep-eep-eep' in a strangely feminine note which drew his mate to the nest on the instant. Handing over immediately, he flew low and fast to a rock at the foot of the valley wall, where the sun, as he perched briefly, lent him the appearance of an over-sized kingfisher. Then away from the valley he went. For fifteen seconds, the hen fixed us with an intent gaze from the topmost spray of the nest-tree. Fears eventually calmed, she crept in to brood. A little dazed by our good fortune, we lowered binoculars and reflected upon the duty which now clearly beckoned.

7

Incubation

The merlins had not, in our opinion, chosen prudently. The moorland at the other end of the hills was more remote, less accessible. But here, there ran a track used by people exercising dogs; by less frequent but more threatening parties of anything up to thirty or so organised hikers. The site was far too near places to which cars might be driven and parked. One could visualise even the possibility of an unusually energetic family party climbing the track to picnic under the very tree. Dogs, noisy children, ball-games; that abomination of abominations, a transistor radio emitting loud and nauseous pop music. White shirts, brightly flowered frocks, screaming children, barking dogs. Not long, perhaps, before 'Ooh! Fred; a funny blue bird's just flown out of that tree. Climb up and see if there's a nest!' The mind was entitled to boggle.

Protection must be organised for week-ends and for the forthcoming bank holiday, at least. Consultations were entered into; various possibilities discussed. A bounty for the farmer who rented the grazing, put up by me and payable when the young had fledged? A fiver a bird, perhaps? My friend on the spot was wise and experienced in such matters. In the absence of financial inducements larger than I could conveniently offer or a force large enough to provide a dawn-to-dusk guard seven days a week, he favoured secrecy coupled with the most discreet of week-end observation, especially if and when the weather promised, or in the circumstances, threatened, to be fine and warm.

On that we decided. Secrecy and discreet local protection based on a cover story good enough to satisfy any but the most thoroughly informed who might ask embarrassing questions. The merlins, if seen and commented on by anyone failing to identify them correctly, would be referred to as 'kestrels', as

Apart from the absence of foliage (the hawthorn had been killed in the interests of conifer afforestation) a typical crows' nest merlin site *(H. McSweeney)*

A merlin on the watch for prey from an observation perch; a habit common to the species *(Dennis Green)*

Patience and application rewarded *(Dennis Green)*

Portrait. The facial beauty of the hen merlin captured to perfection *(H. McSweeney)*

would be their nest if a partially informed intruder found it. The hen should be fairly easy to pass off; we just hoped with fingers crossed that the vivid blue cock would keep out of the way at any time of crisis. If the plan failed to work, we should have to reconsider how money might be used to get the entire area closed to intrusion during the vital weeks. The birds' principal security, we knew, lay in the remarkable deafness and blindness to Nature of the ordinary town-dweller holiday-making in the countryside. What might have to be done to deter a premeditated attempt to steal eggs or nestlings by specialists at the game was another matter. The forces of law and order lay beyond effective summoning. We hardly squared up to the conventional image of vigilantes, but the spirit, at least, was willing.

But the first and by far most important consideration of all was to set up protection in such a way that we ourselves did not pose a threat equal to or greater than those against which we sought to guard. The merlins themselves had by now given pretty clear indications of what they considered tolerable. In short, no more than three people at a time, soberly clad, sitting comparatively still in clear view of the birds but not obtrusively so. The distance: at least 200yd from the nest. Raptors, which may tolerate a full-scale hide at extremely close quarters, are deeply suspicious of people detected while looking as though they attempted concealment. The principle of ambush is one with which they are thoroughly familiar.

As they came to know us better, and they certainly learned to distinguish between people to whom they had grown accustomed and total strangers, the merlins became less suspicious, showing this in several ways. One was to choose to preen on perches quite close to us when there were others, no less suitable, much farther off.

Sentry duty commenced on 14 May. As we approached the site, a merlin was heard calling anxiously. We hastened our footsteps to find, as we came within view, a raven labouring up with the hen merlin manoeuvring into an attacking position. The assault was no less determined than that we had seen delivered on the buzzard by her mate, but the raven appeared to be less impressed. Offering no defence, it accelerated its wing-stroke slightly and quitted the area by the most direct route.

We settled down to watch in weather which improved minute by minute. By 11am the sun shone from a summer sky, but it illuminated no merlin for us. The nest, in which one of the birds was presumed to be incubating eggs, could not be seen through the screen of the foliage. Later observations led to the conclusion that the cock had been in occupation while the hen, observing intrusion from a guard-post on one of the crags, had risen to deal with the raven. Also, that a relief had been overlooked immediately afterwards.

Two hours of inactivity were terminated by merlin calls and the sight of the hen flying from the nest to the tree growing from the rock-face where we had first seen her. The cock orbited the nest-tree in widening circles, then flashed down to ground level while on the far side to glide in fast a few inches above the bilberries and shoot vertically into the branches just when he seemed to be about to ram the trunk with his head. There could hardly be an approach better calculated to obviate detection.

Half an hour later, while the hen was still preening on a nearby rock, two walkers appeared lower down the valley. As they reached a point about 300yd away, she dropped silently from her perch to fly away stealthily; fast and only a foot above the ground, her wing-beat rapid and shallow. The strangers walked on and out of the valley, unaware of the gaze, avian and human, bent suspiciously upon them. Forty minutes later, the hen returned, displaying briefly over the adjacent moorland before entering the valley to perch in the top of the nest-tree. She 'eep-eeped' plaintively; not, perhaps, the best of ways to avoid attracting attention. The cock vacated the nest, displayed energetically over the heather and muted copiously, thus informing us that his stint, by the standards of his internal economy, had been a prolonged one.

This time, the hen sat for just over an hour. The usual babble of conversation signalled the change-over when it came. No more than fifteen minutes after the cock had settled down, the hen returned, flew to the top of the nest-tree and tried to call him off the eggs. He stubbornly declined to stir, from which we deduced that the instinct to incubate may be encouraged by some pleasure derived from doing it. Disconsolately, she continued to call, but to no avail. Eventually discouraged, the hen flew to a favourite perch, preened, scratched her chin with a talon (a most hazardous-looking operation) and stretched first her left wing, then her right. After preening again, she raised a foot slowly, scrutinised it and clenched her talons. Raptors often seem thus preoccupied with the source of their designation.

Half an hour later, after a spell of renewed calling in which the plaintive 'eep-eep-eep' developed gradually into the more strident 'airt-airt-airt', she flew straight and fast to the tree to perch in a position which allowed her to stare full into the face of her mate. Anxious screams were interspersed with whinnying cries not unlike the usual note of the kestrel, or, as we were later to hear, the cries made by merlin nestlings when they discover their voices. Obediently, this time, the cock surrendered tenure. This stint, too lasted for an hour, but the precise circumstances of the relief, when it came, were lost in a confusion of rapid movement. This was disappointing, but no occasion for special complaint on a merlin site, as we were destined to discover all too frequently.

At 6.15pm we left with food for thought. Incubation was less of a chore than we had supposed it would be. Greater still was our surprise at discovering that birds might find it a positive pleasure. But what controlled the timing of reliefs? One might have expected the decision to be made and signalled by a bird grown cramped and bored, begging for relief. No such thing. The return to provide relief was voluntary and at the initiative of the relieving bird.

Just how far either flew from the vicinity of the nest we had not established, the lie of the land being unhelpful, but the earlier sighting of the hen from the moorland pool a mile and a half from the valley gave an indication. Often, she remained in view of us and the nest for some time after relief. In contrast, the cock almost invariably flew right out of sight with the minimum of delay, but later, we were to learn from the speed at which he might return in the event of trouble that he did not usually at this stage fly very far away unless it was forced upon him in the course of searching for prey.

Our arrival at the foot of the hill on 21 May was heralded by the cock merlin flying close by the car as we donned gum-boots and waterproofs, calling attention noisily to his presence. A mile from the site, there was temptation to anthropomorphise it into a greeting. It was, in truth, a strange incident. Birds of prey are notorious for a strong inclination to silence away from the nest site. Greeting it was not: but it might, for all that, have implied recognition. He was heading for the low-lying farmlands and it therefore came as no surprise when we arrived at the rim of the valley to find chaffinch and yellowhammer remains newly added to the piles of pipit feathers on the plucking-post. Two chaffinches, a yellowhammer, a whinchat, a skylark, a cock wheatear, a cock ring ousel and twenty-five meadow pipits had suffered conversion. Perhaps the presence of feathers from the birds caught away from the moor indicated a thinning out of the latter.

The wearing of waterproofs had been no idle precaution. Although the day was windy, cloud and drizzle obscured the skylines. Little likelihood of casual intruders, but not much of successful bird watching either, with raindrops blurring both spectacle lenses and binoculars. We settled down to our duty in a spirit of grim resolution. After all, if egg thieves knew of the site, there could hardly be a more propitious occasion for their purpose. Merlins came and went; notes (of a sort) were made. The only thing to be established clearly was that the nest was still tenanted.

Not that the day was entirely without interest. Because of a 180° change in the direction of the wind, we watched from a sheltered spot farther down the valley than before, and made the acquaintance of a fresh community of small birds. Despite the inclemency of the weather, there was considerable activity.

A fine cock ring ousel flew up into a rowan by the stream, sang what he fancied to be a song and exhibited himself boldly. A pair of redstarts, seen in the valley for the first time, flitted in and out of a thorn growing from the rock: a pair of whinchats disputed possession of our new OP. The redstarts' thorn-bush and several others were now in blossom; the valley smelt fresh and fragrant in the rain.

Between 5 and 6pm the rain finally ceased. The hen merlin celebrated the fact with a brief soaring flight, after which she landed in the top of a bush already occupied by a cock blackbird. Blackie was thrown into confusion; three impulses in conflict. One; to remove himself expeditiously from the vicinity of the falcon. Second; to cling to the refuge offered by cover. Third; to defend his territory, at the heart of which stood the bush in which he had been surprised. The third impulse came near to triumphing, such is the influence of territory on birds. He puffed out his feathers and clucked aggressively. Then with evident second thoughts, he hopped to an outside twig, flexed his legs, flirted his tail and flicked his wings as though about to fly. The merlin, turning her head, regarded him calmly. Blackie retired to the fastnesses of his bush, giving vent to further indignant clucks. Thus, conflicting impulses were reconciled with a manifestation of something very like an intelligent compromise.

In the event, Blackie stimulated but the faintest interest on the merlin's part, a fact which added fuel to a small fire which had been smouldering in my mind all day. It had been kindled by observations of the remarkable number of small birds coexistent in this valley with the merlins. Earlier experiences were called to mind: impressions planted originally by a pair of kestrels which shared in 1946 a Cyrenaican water-tower nest site with a colony of house sparrows. Kestrels, of course, are not bird-eaters to any notable extent; their preference is for furred game. This fact had blurred a conclusion which might at that time have been reached. The issue was clearer now that merlins were the raptors involved.

Was there, perhaps, some evolutionary factor at work which

gave survival-value to the practice in raptors of refraining from the slaughter of their immediate neighbours? It could hardly be a matter of concealment. Having made their kills away from home, both merlin and sparrowhawk, I knew, brought them back to the vicinity of the nest for rough-plucking. What, then? Could it be that raptors which practised this restraint through the ages through which they had figured among the earth's fauna, fortuitously bequeathed to their newly fledged and inexperienced progeny an advantage in the form of a territory, well stocked with potential prey, which had grown dangerously familiar with the presence of raptors? Of one thing bearing directly on this question I was reasonably sure. Parent birds 'driving away' their young when they had reached the age of independence was largely or wholly a myth. In the case of many species, the reverse is often – perhaps always – the case. The territory is handed over, temporarily, at least, to the new generation without conflict. It is the parents which withdraw, if only for the time being.

Thus it follows that a dense population of relatively unwary prey could confer great advantage on a young merlin freshly embarked upon its career. Practice makes perfect; but something is needed to practise on and little is learned from consistent failure. Failure teaches something; but success, too, is needed to round out experience and complete the picture. If the eggs hatched and the young survived to fledge, time would perhaps shed more light on this question.

After a thorough preen to groom plumage a little bedraggled by persistent drizzle, the hen merlin left the bush to perform a prolonged soaring flight over the valley, concluded by fast circling and turns almost too tight for the eye to follow. Having worked off surplus energy (and gloom engendered by a miserably wet day?) she flew low and fast towards what we supposed to be her personal hunting preserve. An hour later, we heard her call and saw her rising rapidly towards a buzzard high over the head of the valley. After a 'ranging' stoop, she outclimbed it swiftly to reach a pitch 100ft above that at which it calmly soared. Tilting over, the merlin closed her wings right into her body and fell headlong at it. The buzzard evaded her with a paroxysmal twisting jink. Like an arrowhead she continued to fall, flattening out but a few feet above the heather to speed into dead ground.

Her mate brooded on, indifferent to the chilly world beyond the rim of the warm nest.

8

The Final Days

The weekend of the 27th/28th was the bank holiday we feared above all other hazards. We greeted with relief the howling north-wester which ushered it in and the fierce spit of cold rain it bore. The appropriate OP for the day gave a view right into the nest, intermittently, as the wild wind tossed even the stiff branches of the thorn tree to and fro. The hen merlin sat tight. Voicing a hope that she was not subject to *mal de mer*, I settled down to watch and ward.

After half an hour, she moved; giving the impression that she turned the eggs. Several times in the next four and a half hours she moved. Four and a half hours grew into five, but still no relief. Had the cock come to grief? As far as we knew, the moor, although stocked with grouse and shot over, was keepered unintensively. Neither was there real suspicion that the keeper would harm the merlins if he should discover them. Could it be that as the end of incubation approached, the hen took over the bulk of the burden? Had Nature contrived some way of arranging this so that the mother should be the bird present when the eggs actually hatched? It seemed not improbable.

The sky cleared, the wind moved round a few points and increased in ferocity. Our sheltered spot became less so, causing us to move to where we lost sight of the nest and the sitting bird. Now, we sat in the mouth of one of the small gullies which broke the valley wall.

Suddenly, there was a rush of wings. The cock merlin, returning to the scene by way of that very gully, had come within an ace of removing my hat. Shocked and for the moment at a loss, he banked steeply and hung stalled in a gust of wind 6ft from the end of my nose. With every feather spread, he looked spectacularly handsome, the features standing out most prominently, the broad black subterminal bar drawn boldly across an otherwise unmarked slate-blue tail. Regaining control, he flew swiftly downwind and out of sight. Ten minutes later, I caught a glimpse of him ghosting in to the foot of the nest-tree, using its trunk to screen his approach from us. He came extremely fast; and for once, in complete silence. He flew straight to the nest, without perching beforehand at all.

Summarily, he ejected his mate from the eggs. She tumbled from the tree, dazed and stupified. At its foot, there was a stone about the size of a domestic hen's egg. Edging herself forward on her carpal joints, she settled down to brood it for the whole of ten minutes. Gradually, she recovered her wits and slicked down her puffed-out feathers. From an experience of domestic poultry, I would hazard a guess that the chilling wind was the reviving factor. She lifted her wings to it and was picked up like a puff of swansdown. Away she went to perch low in the heather in the area of the thorn growing from the cliff which she so often favoured. With a flutter of wings, she stepped down behind a heather clump, out of sight and out of the wind. A few minutes later she left, flying away downwind faster than ever.

In an hour, she was back; calling the cock peremptorily off the eggs. He obeyed instantly. Two hours later, the gale had blown itself out and the first buzzard of the day was up. A raven accompanied it, the two birds counter-circling in harmony. There was no interference from the cock merlin, presumably too far away to be aware of what was going on over his own valley. Twenty minutes later, he returned, landed on the rim of the cliffs and called sharply. The hen came straight off the nest, flew to and hovered briefly above him, closed her wings to make a pass at him, then flew away over the moor.

The cock sat on his perch for several minutes, then flew to the tree, hovered briefly over the nest, dropped to the eggs. Soon, a strange *sotto voce* screaming was audible. It continued for half an hour. Had an egg hatched? The time must be drawing near. As it transpired, the cock himself was the source of the sound. Perhaps he responded to other sounds beginning to emanate from within one or more of the eggs.

It was now time to go. Walking along the rim of the valley, I saw the hen coming in. She flew to a perch 100yd along the rocks. I moved closer, slowly. She stood her ground. Through the glasses I could see that she watched me intently. I sat. Promptly, she flew to the nest, perching briefly on the topmost spray of the tree. The cock emerged, dropped to the ground beneath; the setting sun illuminating his vivid colours. Taking off, he flew into it; to land on a solitary dead twig poking up from the distant heather at the head of the valley. The final view that evening was of his silhouette, black against the golden sunset.

By the following morning, the wind was back in the south-west, with a desultory drizzle falling from scudding grey cloud. I arrived at the site to find the cock on the nest, the faint screaming ceased.

After a quarter of an hour, a sheep moved towards the tree, putting up off the ground a brown bird previously unnoticed. Perched low in a small dead thorn, it proved to be the hen merlin. After preening, she flew to her usual perch in the topmost spray of the nest-tree to call the cock off the eggs. He complied promptly, leaving the valley before his mate had settled down to her task. Rain began to fall in earnest: the ring ousel pair grew noisy. Presumably, there was some connection.

The rain did not, in fact, develop into the downpour expected; but was heavy enough to keep the moor and the valley clear of visitors for the best part of the day.

At 2.40pm, there were merlin calls but no sighting. At 2.45 and again at 3; but no relief took place. By now, although convinced that the nest still contained only eggs, I wondered whether the apparent reluctance of the hen to accept relief meant that hatching was imminent. At 3.30, after conversation between the birds, she at last acquiesced, leaving the nest by a course which took her to the heather beyond the head of the valley. As she landed, a disturbed raven beat up into the air.

The cock took off and circled up, laboriously in the heavy air, the raven easily out-climbing him. The hen remained on her perch in the heather. Two carrion crows alighted on the rocks down-valley. With the eggs uncovered, tension mounted. For five minutes, the cock circled the valley chattering, with the hen screaming harshly from her perch below. The crows ventured nearer: the cock departed without the least attempt to deal with them. The hen returned to the nest, still screaming raucously. Gradually, her cries subsided. The crows fled quietly away, having seen something still hidden from our eyes.

The 'something' was a party of ten assorted adults and children, accompanied by three dogs over which no control whatsoever was exercised. As they strolled slowly up-valley, the dogs fanned out in a screen before them, putting to flight every sheep and lamb within sight. The lapwings fled; so did the curlews. Also the ring ousels, the redstarts, the whinchats. Within three minutes, the valley had been emptied of its indigenous animal life – except for the hen merlin sitting tight on her so-far unobserved nest.

A child carried a ball; a young woman cuddled a transistor radio blaring out tinny electronic sound. They gathered beneath the nest-tree and sought places to sit. The sun selected this of all times to emerge from behind the clouds and shine warmly. I tightened my grip on my stout limewood staff, conflicting thoughts and plans chasing each other through my mind. Be frank without being explicit? There was something about these people which discouraged the prospect. Impersonate authority and order them off? Merely silly. Now the crisis had come, I was caught miserably in two minds. Thoughts grew wilder. Stroll over with a winning smile on my face and warn them of entirely fictitious poisonous snakes? Perhaps the best idea yet.

But greater powers had the matter in hand. A black cloud raced up to obscure the sun: down came a harsh scatter of pea-sized rain-drops: a sudden wind howled in the hawthorns. In less time than it takes to tell, the invasion was over; the enemy in full retreat, routed by the only known rival to Russia's 'General Winter' . . . the British summer. And I hadn't been obliged to make a fool of myself after all.

The intruders had come from two caravans which a farmer,

for a few shillings a night, had allowed to be parked on his land. I hope the condition lost by his sheep and lambs in the mad gallop inspired by the questing dogs did not exceed the value of the 'let'. As I watched through the binoculars while most of them ran a mile before halting for breath, I wouldn't have bet on it.

All through the disturbance, the hen merlin sat tight. We wondered anxiously what the outcome would have been had the arrival of the invading army coincided with the confused situation prevailing after the departing hen merlin had put up the raven. Just how long merlin eggs could be left unbrooded at this stage in their development, we did not know, but common sense suggested that the period could not be indefinite. The hen still sat unrelieved when we left.

On the following morning, more rain threatened: nothing of note occurred. At 1.00pm the threat was made good. We and the likelihood of further disturbing human intrusion were rained off together. At this stage, we thought, the danger from professional egg-thieves should be over. They must know that by now the eggs would be too far advanced in incubation to be of value to them.

Two days later, chance presented an unexpected opportunity to spend an evening with the merlins. The nest, however, appeared to be deserted. Then a ring ousel began to sing from the top of a neighbouring tree and the redstart pair to potter about in the lower branches. Then the cock redstart fluttered up to the top of the merlins' tree and looked down into the nest. To my immense relief, a head with a steely blue hooked bill and two big dark eyes was raised to stare back. The shocked redstart stood his ground, defying the merlin with a stream of abuse. She disdaining to notice him, he withdrew eventually in safety.

Time went by: the hen merlin grew visibly restless. A fresh wind sprang up, depressing the temperature of a hitherto warm evening uncomfortably. The ring ousels continued activity; the redstarts explored everything in view, myself, a less hazardous target for their abuse, included. At 8.00pm, when I was on the point of departure, the cock arrived and took over. His mate testified to the length of her unrelieved sojourn by the copiousness of her mute as she flew from the tree. As she alighted on a rock to stretch cramped limbs and preen, two soberly dressed people accompanied by an orderly spaniel entered the valley. No peace for the wicked: nor much for the innocent. The hen flew silently away; the cock sat tight and motionless. After watching the harmless strollers safely out of the valley, I, too, left the scene.

9

Hatching

The eggs hatched on 10 June, during our enforced absence for a fortnight. The merlin pair, so the man on the spot later informed me, proved to be excellent parents from the outset, the best he had ever watched. The cock was a successful and hard-working hunter, bringing kills in abundance to the nest; the hen brooded the newly hatched nestlings with the maximum of conceivable assiduity. Prey was brought rough-plucked by the cock to the rocks on the rim of the valley to be surrendered to the hen for final delivery. For the first few days, she tore from it tiny fragments of breast and thigh meat, eating the coarser portions herself. Gradually larger pieces, including feathers and quite substantial bones, were fed to the fast-growing nestlings.

By 24 June, when we at last caught up with the situation, they were half grown and had exchanged their first coat of white down for another of smoky blue, tinged brown. They looked remarkably large as they scrambled round the crows' nest, jockeying for the most comfortable positions and snapping at the flies which had begun to torment them. Their appetites seemed insatiable. Birds, all of them apparently meadow pipits, were brought to the nest at 11.30, 11.50, 12.55, 1.10, 1.40, 2.55 and 6.00. At 1.30 also, the hen paid a visit, but on that occasion there was failure to establish whether prey was carried. At each presentation, all three youngsters clamoured frantically, however recently one or more of them had been fed. The arrival of a parent was greeted with thin screaming on a cracked note; actual presentation of food was accompanied by throaty 'tyuk-tyuk-tyuk' calls. Appreciative though they sounded, we failed to discover at that stage whether they had been uttered by parent or offspring. Later, we learned that they were in fact the parental command to open bills and accept what was thrust in.

The main burden of the hunting was borne by the male, who acquitted himself well on a morning of drizzle and damp still air. But not the whole burden. Scanning with the binoculars during the late afternoon, I picked up a merlin comparatively high over the moor at the head of the valley. It was the hen, in hot pursuit of a meadow pipit; one, I supposed, of a pair actually resident at the very top of the valley. What, I wondered did that signify – that pressure had so thinned out the less wary specimens on the usual hunting-ranges that kills on the doorstep were now enforced by necessity? It was certainly the first time that anything of this kind had been seen.

The pipit, no tyro, gave the impression that evasion of merlin attacks was all part of a normal day's work. The merlin's technique differed from anything encountered in falconry literature. She did not attempt to 'fly the bird down, following and imitating every jink, twist and deflection', as the books usually state, but behaved more like a peregrine in miniature. The pipit was pursued and attacked by a series of short, shallow stoops, in which the merlin used the momentum generated to fling up after each evasion to a pitch sufficient for the launching of the next. There was no frantic effort to close and grapple. When the pipit dodged successfully, as it did again and again, the merlin either rose sharply to dive immediately, or circled in a more gradual ascending banked glide as a preliminary to making the next stoop from farther off, initiating the attack with a few fast wing-beats.

It was impossible to see how the pipit continued to escape her. Time and again, the two silhouettes merged into one. Surely the grasping talons must close on the small bird, by now inevitably grown weary? The pipit faltered; succumbing to a temptation to change its intention in mid-manoeuvre. A foot shot out: a few tiny feathers danced on the breeze. But it was not the end. The pipit climbed away from the falcon like a minute rocket: the merlin broke off her attack, deceiving me – the pipit too, perhaps – into supposing that she had abandoned it finally. The pipit, now high over the valley, began to drop towards the ground.

By now, the merlin was 200yd downwind, climbing gradually in a wide circle. As her altitude reached that of the descending pipit she tipped over at a steeply banked angle and beat her wings powerfully about fifteen times. Then, shrugging them into her sides for the first and only time in the encounter, she swept in like Nemesis, not so very steeply, but at an extraordinary speed. It seemed that the pipit remained unaware of her return until she came within grasping distance. Whether what followed was intentional or salvation by accident as the small bird fainted with terror, I cannot say, but it, too, closed its wings and fell to the ground like a stone.

There was no attempt to follow it. The merlin broke instead into level wingbeat-driven flight and pitched in the top of a tall straggling hawthorn at the head of the valley. Perching at first typically upright, she then adopted a strange horizontal posture, staring into the sky and performing odd bowing movements. What she saw with the naked eye, I failed to find with 12-power binoculars. At the time, I wondered whether she had in fact seen anything. From experience since widened, I now know it to have been another female of her own species, crossing the territory at immense height. Her strange bowings and writhings were an invitation to her mate, wherever he might be, to copulate; the invariable response of a female falcon whose conjugal jealousy has been aroused by fears of sexual competition. As this reaction may be witnessed long after copulation can serve any direct reproductive purpose, its implications provide much food for thought on animal and human behaviour and the size of the distinctions between them which some people still draw.

Eventually, the hen merlin left; to return at 5.15 pm, carrying prey. This she bore for plucking to an ant-hill. A rain of feathers drifted down. Then she fed. Afterwards, she preened. Then she left the valley, returning a few minutes before 6.00 to make the last food presentation we saw that day. An hour and a half later, we left.

The day had produced much of interest: carriage and presentation of food, for example. Kills destined for the nestlings had their tails and wing-quills removed before delivery; were carried to the tree in the talons, as might be expected, but transferred to the bill before the adult bird disappeared into the foliage by the nest. Then there was the matter of brooding. In nine hours, apart from a possibility at 1.30, the young had not been brooded, unless for a few minutes only immediately after feeding: this despite the fact that they were still in down and the day anything but warm. Thought was stimulated on thermal efficiency, insulation and the remarkable efficacy of down. Merlin nestlings were, after all, very small creatures for whom conservation of body-heat must represent a specially important issue. Thought, too, was provoked on merlin appetite and its likely effect on bird population in general. We may well have been watching just when the food demand of the nestlings was at its absolute peak. Bearing in mind the hours of daylight during which we were not present, the total daily kill was likely to reach or exceed a dozen birds. The young would be in the nest for about a month. The adults had been on the moor since mid-April. If all went well, from some date in mid-July until the end of September there would be five hungry merlins on the moor – though less hungry, perhaps, than growing nestlings.

So far, we had not discerned any reduction in the numbers of small birds on the moor. Either the depradations were spread too widely to be noticed, or the reproductive efforts of the pipits in particular were making good the casualties virtually as they took place. What, we wondered, would the situation be in September? Perhaps we should gain first-hand data bearing on the vexed question of whether prey controlled predators or predators prey. I suspected that the true answer would prove less facile than implied by the question when put in such terms.

Our next visit was made a week later, on 1 July. The day was cool, with banked cloud drifting across a sky which cleared sufficiently from time to time for the sun to break through and complicate matters with heat haze. Haze attributable more to the state of the ground than air temperature, despite the date.

Activity in the nest and our arrival coincided. The nestlings had grown well during the week and feathered up to a surprising extent. Now, they were distinctly brown, the smoky down reduced to mere patches. I lowered the glasses in a glow of satisfaction. If we could but escape a raid during the next seven days, reasonable hopes might be cherished of seeing three more merlins recruited into the exiguous Welsh population.

Then my eye fell on something at the foot of the tree. Brown, roughly the shape of a bird, absolutely motionless. Every stick and stone usually at the foot of the tree were familiar. I did not like the look of the situation. Scrambling down the rocks, I walked over. One of the young merlins lay dead; still warm, not yet in rigor mortis. It was plump and without flaw with not a hint of injury beyond blood in its bill which might have come from prey consumed earlier that morning. Had we arrived an hour sooner, we might have been in time to save it. The fact that the development shown by flight and tail quills indicated the bird to be within only days of flying was an added irony. I pocketed the body and walked back to the OP, the day suddenly colder and duller.

As I did so, the hen was seen to leave the tree. She had been there while I retrieved her dead nestling, making not a murmur of protest. My local friend had seen another hen at another time feed and brood a nestling which survived such a fall. So a nestling, merely by falling, did not in its mother's eyes lose identity. Death as a fact must be recognised by merlins as it is recognised by us.

If the merlin suffered distress at the death of her infant, her recovery was mercifully swift. Two survivors with continuing demands to be met may have accounted for that. She returned to the nest an hour later, to deliver a complete meadow pipit to the remaining occupants. Wing and tail quills had, as usual, been removed, but no attempt at dismemberment followed. She came in without a sound. In the tree, nothing was audible beyond a brief 'tuk-tukking' before the prey was surrendered. Afterwards, she sat motionless as a museum specimen for half an hour, perched in the top of a belatedly blossoming hawthorn a hundred yards farther up the valley. Immediately after her departure, the cock arrived, calling. When discovered, he sat on a tussock with an unusually large golden-brown bird held in his bill. His bill: not his talons. A skylark. His mate returned, stooped at him, put him up, accompanied him out of sight beyond the skyline. The noise grew to incessant clamour, all four birds contributing. Skylarks, it seemed, were something special. The clamour reached a crescendo. I focused on the tree just in time to see the cock emerge, his journey in accomplished unobserved. As he left, so the hen alighted, to remove the skylark just deposited. Juvenile wails of protest re-echoed round the valley. Flying to her plucking post, the hen bent to her task. Our first impression was of simple larceny. Unprincipled: unmaternal to a shocking degree; but simple. We were wrong. Having divested the kill of the stiff flight and tail quills which father had thought suitable diet for 21-day-olds, she carried the lark back to them without, so far as we could judge, purloining so much as a single billfull.

A recollection of the dried blood in the throat of the dead nestling struck home with force. Had we, perhaps, received a clue to the mystery? To retrieve something from the loss, I sent the body to Nature Conservancy for autopsy. Analysis, by revealing organochlorine residues or their absence, would tell much of the health of the small birds on which the young merlins had been fed and thus of future prospects, but delays in the post frustrated even this intention: a bluebottle had discovered the body before I did.

The day continued to prove eventful. At 2.30 in the afternoon, both nestlings climbed on to the edge of the nest to exercise their wings. At 3.00, while exercise continued, albeit a trifle obscured by foliage, a brown bundle fluttered to the ground. What do we do now? The tree was dense and thorny; the nest high in its branches. All options seemed equally discouraging. The 'bundle' gathered itself, looked in all directions, leaped into the air and flashed away up-valley as fast as an arrow. The hen, arriving unobserved, had departed with less than her accustomed dignity. We breathed again.

Shortly afterwards, we left; walking via the line of plucking posts, now extended to include part of the track which was a public right of way. Pipit feathers were littered everywhere; there was the bill and face of a skylark, remains of whinchat, wheatear and ring ousel; an absolute shambles. Half an hour was spent in removing this mass of tell-tale evidence before it attracted unwelcome attention. We left the valley surmising correctly that when next we saw the nestlings, they would be 'nestlings' no longer.

10
Adolescence

8 July was hazy and humid. As we walked up the edge of the valley, the hen merlin took off from a heather-spray and left at high speed. The man on the spot had checked on the 6th, finding the young birds still in the nest but beyond doubt almost – ready to go. We found the nest empty; likewise, we thought, the valley. The silence was absolute. So it remained for more than an hour.

Suddenly, clamour rang out on all sides. There seemed to be merlins everywhere; yikking, screaming, squeeping hoarsely, in accordance with age and sex. Confusion reigned over all. Then, its elements began to unravel. To our right, a brown merlin flew at and buzzed a small thorn tree, directing thereby our attention to the male who sat high in its branches, chattering at the top of his voice. Immediately, he took off; to fly, followed by her, to the rocks two hundred yards up the valley. The squeeping on our left rose to a crescendo. From behind a rock buttress, which had hidden them since our arrival, stepped the two young merlins. The valley had not, after all, been so empty as it had seemed. So, whatever the future might hold in store, the fledglings had survived the first critical hours out of the nest.

No falconer, as well-informed as us but cleverer, had crept in at first or last light to carry out a well-planned raid. No fox, stoat or polecat had lain in wait for the conclusion of the first fluttering, uncertain, flight. No child had been present to capture the quickly exhausted bird before the full use of its wings had been gained, to carry it proudly away to where it would pine away its brief life, grasping a dowell perch in a budgerigar's cage, trying without success to digest pigeon corn or thrive on chopped earthworms. Large mercies; meriting appropriate thanks.

The next question; how well could they fly *now*? It was answered within a minute or two by a surprisingly strong flight to the rocks up-valley, followed by a touch-down under more than fair control. First by one bird, then by the other; both squeaking anxiously until reunion had been accomplished.

As the morning wore on, the parents came and went, sometimes with prey, at others without. The youngsters remained in sight, engaged for much of the time in removing the last traces of down from their plumage. At 1.30, rain set in: cold rain which increased to winter-like ferocity. The young merlins reacted hardly at all. After an hour's drenching, one moved to a perch half in shelter where it slept, head tucked into scapularies. The other continued to perch where it was wholly exposed to the elements, as though hypnotised by the driving rain. Soon, the feathers of both were saturated and bedraggled. Our 'waterproofs' serving us not a great deal better, we retreated, chilled and low in spirits. So much effort: so much luck. Might all be brought to nought by a freak turn in the weather?

It was not. Early next morning I returned. High cotton-wool clouds drifted across a warm blue sky. The day was fresh as April and as full of promise. Two young merlins sat on the rocks, still plucking down. Not a cough; not a sneeze. Not a hint of droopiness. Bright of eye, every feather in place. Merlins, it appeared, were made of pretty stern stuff.

Throughout the morning, they sunned themselves and preened, often plucking remnants of down from each other's plumage. They also displayed more sophisticated powers of flight than I had expected in birds so recently on the wing. Journeys of two hundred yards and more were made; concluded by highly professional circling over the proposed point of touch-down and a remarkably accurate final glide-in. I was right to be surprised. Later experience confirmed that such aptitude was not automatic.

They were fed at frequent intervals, but that did not prevent them from importuning passing woodpigeons also for food.

Later observations confirmed there to be nothing unusual in this. Newly-fledged merlins allege parenthood at every flying object equal to or exceeding their own size, up to and including piston aircraft if they fly low. Jets alone may inspire fear – or the nearest thing to it of which a merlin is capable.

At 1.10, the male brought in prey; again at 1.20, at 2.25 and at 3.15. The hen, too, made visits, but never to bring food. She, it seemed, had declared a public holiday for one; a proceeding which failed signally to win the approval of her offspring. The 2.25 presentation struck a new note. Flashing in at tremendous speed, the cock stooped at the surprised youngsters on their perch, zoomed up high, tore away up-valley. Only after his departure was the object of his visit explained by one of the young birds standing crouched over the kill.

The merlin concluded his display by falling like an arrowhead into the gorge from which he had risen. His progeny remained oblivious to their sire's aerobatic feats. One continued to feed, the other to register protest. Strong though the sibling-bond undoubtedly was, it did not extend to the voluntary sharing of prey. Next, the hen visited the scene, again with nothing in her talons. From the wild chase and scrimmage which ensued in the heather, it seemed that she herself was destined to stand substitute for her omission. Eventually, disengagement was accomplished and the young returned to their rock, appetite unsated but distress abated with Mother out of sight.

Later in the afternoon, they began to search heather clumps for insects and were seen to enjoy some success. In the course of this there was an occasion when some dispute of ownership led to a falling out and squaring up, fighting-cock style. Tempers cooling as quickly as they had risen, it came to nothing. Gradually, the tempo of the day grew slower: less flying, less preening, less investigation of the heather. Finally, the young birds perched recumbently, like domestic poultry or ducks. Soon we withdrew; the valley at peace and filled with golden evening sunshine.

A week passed; the sands of time were now low in the hourglass. On 16 July the question was whether we should see the merlins at all rather than what they might next do for our entertainment and instruction. Searching through reference books had not enlightened us how long fledged merlins remained in the vicinity of their hatching, but much, it might be supposed, would depend on terrain. The valley formed an incomparable natural nursery: so far we had not seen them leave its confines. Hopeful as the birdwatcher must always be, but nevertheless half in expectation of finding the valley abandoned, we approached it; this time from the moor above.

Such optimism as we had mustered was immediately justified. From 400yd away, a merlin could be seen perched bolt upright on a straggling spray of dead heather. But which member of the family? As we drew nearer it became clear that the bird was more brown than blue; the typical 'plummy' colour of the juvenile in its first plumage while that plumage is still fresh and unfaded by the sun's rays. It watched us approach to within a hundred yards, then flew; vanishing into a fold in the ground in classic fashion. Fine. But had *both* survived their first full week out in the world, we wondered?

By now, we were on the rim of the valley, seeking the path which led down. From a rock-ledge immediately below, a young merlin took off, chattering with anger at the disturbance to proper enjoyment of its elevenses, the unexpired portion of which it carried to a perch farther along the rocks. The survival question was answered there and then by the other flying from where it had perched unseen among the rocks to the top of a tall hawthorn in the valley bottom. There was now little distinction to be drawn between the flight-style of adult and juvenile.

We moved on to our chosen OP while the second young merlin sampled various perches on trees and bushes along the stream, and on the rocks. The other, having finished its interrupted meal, flew to the rocks at the head of the valley, where it settled down to preen. Thus preoccupied, it was caught completely off guard by the sudden stoop of a mature cock kestrel which had drifted over with deceptive innocence, high above the valley. The young merlin, although knocked sprawling and squeaking from its perch, lost no time in recovering and launching a counter-attack. The assault was pressed furiously home: the kestrel fled. Its erstwhile victim hung ruthlessly on its tail; the other young merlin overtook them fast, obviously determined not to be left out of the fun. All vanished over the skyline, the merlins shooting up into the sky overhead a few seconds later to practise vigorously what we came to call 'fighter tactics'.

Using each other as targets, they experimented with the performance and evasion of every aerial ploy in the merlin's considerable repertoire; all at high speed and with well-nigh incredible agility. After watching their play for five totally breath-taking minutes, their victory over a bird of a slightly larger species and at least two years their senior was far less astonishing.

The next three hours were marked by continuous activity. Noisy flights from perch to perch; bouts of fighter tactics; preening; the searching of heather clumps for the insects they might contain. The sibling bond remarked earlier had not yet in any way weakened. Either bird might take off and fly to the far end of the valley alone, but if the other was slow to accompany it, there would be clamour until it did. At 2.15 there occurred an incident of special interest and possibly wide implication. Unfortunately, it took place at such a speed that the eye could not be certain that it had not suffered deception. At one moment, both young birds sat preening, relaxed and quiet. The next, there were two merlins in flight, both brown rather than blue, one circling and calling, the other twisting and flashing in pursuit of something not clearly seen. Within another second or two, one stood mantling prey, the other begging to be fed. Both were then seen to be the youngsters. Several constructions may be put upon the matter. Either the initiative was taken by one to hunt – and kill – a pipit or other small bird venturing unwisely into the valley: or a small bird was herded in for the purpose by the hen: or a small bird was live-caught by the hen, and carried in and released before them to stimulate the hunting instinct. The speed and agility of the merlin is a joy to the eye: but it can also prove frustrating to observation.

While eating the kill, the merlin in possession was challenged by a pair of carrion crows. One confronted it; the other took station to the rear to distract it from defence of its property by an attack on its tail feathers, than which there is no more typically corvine trick. The young merlin screamed in protest, looking round the valley as though in hopes of summoning succour. Since none was forthcoming, it grasped the remains of its prey, and flew directly and deliberately towards us to perch on a rock but 30yd away, where it finished its meal in peace. The wary crows, observing our presence, did not follow. Tempted though one must be to credit the merlin with an extraordinary display of sagacity, I think its choice of haven was fortuitous. One thing, though, was established beyond question. To the merlin, a small group of familiar and relatively immobile human beings were neighbours more acceptable than carrion crows.

Having finished its meal and picked its talons clean, the bird returned to the far side of the amphitheatre, flying up to the top of a tall thorn. The crows, which had remained on a rocky vantage-point overlooking this tree, took off silently and approached with stealth. Whether the young merlin was knocked from the tree or fell from it to avoid the blow, cannot with certainty be said; but it fell squeaking and sprawling just as the other had when surprised by the kestrel earlier in the day. But its sibling, perched in another tree 200yd away down-valley, had seen the crows take off and followed suit on the instant.

As the crows had taken the young merlin by surprise, so their turn now came. In the selfsame second that the leading crow attacked the one merlin, the other closed rapidly on crow number two in a fast and determined stoop. Wrenching away as its target twisted out of reach of the outstretched talons, attention was transferred to the leading aggressor, which it buzzed with determination again and again as it sped from the valley, broad black wings flailing faster and faster in a vain attempt to outfly the punishment it had invited.

Both crows having been seen off with a vengeance, the victor joined its ill-used companion where it now sat on the rock from which the crows had launched their assault. For an hour or more, the young merlins sat together, appearing to draw comfort from contiguity.

Suddenly, there was an explosion of screaming and chattering and both young merlins were in flight, coming towards us fast. Directly overhead, 50ft or so above us, circled the adult pair, the cock carrying a pipit dangling enticingly from one foot. After dropping it on the rocks to our left, where the young birds were soon to be engaged in a noisy tug-of-war, he turned into the wind to hang directly over us, head bent and turning in attentive scrutiny. The hen flew in wide circles, screaming raucously, while the cock banked in tight arcs, evidently disinclined to abandon his study. He, previously by far the shyest member of the family, had at last come to accept us as part of the scenery but not devoid of interest. One young merlin mantled and tore at the food; the other squealed disconsolately.

And that was almost the end of the story. It was certainly our final sighting of the adult pair. A week later, our arrival disturbed one young merlin, which departed without haste but did not return. Eight hours of meticulous observation established a number of facts thought to be relevant. There were no fresh feathers on the plucking posts: ravens, kestrels, crows and buzzards had resumed undisputed tenure of the valley. Most significant of all, the population of small birds was noticeably reduced. No redstarts, no whinchats, no ring ousels. Just one pair of meadow pipits, including, I believe, the bird which escaped from the hen merlin that memorable day. It seemed as though the 'well-stocked larder' theory might hold water. The state of the plucking area did not necessarily contradict this, there being no special reason, so far as we could judge, why the young birds should carry their kills there. Bracken now grown thick and tall over much of the amphitheatre might have hidden many a pile of feathers.

From the arrival of the adult pair on the moor to the departure of the family at the end of the summer, something like 450 small birds had died in their talons or were destined so to die in the next few weeks. Was the impact noticeable? I think it was. There was no dramatic shortage of small birds at the end of July, but the marked superabundance to be seen before the merlins hatched their eggs was no longer there.

Perhaps the merlins had in truth done no more than reduce a population mercifully to what the coming winter could support, bringing swift and sudden death to small birds destined otherwise to die miserably of the combined and interrelated effects of cold and starvation, or to breed progeny destined at one or more removes to suffer that fate. The precise pattern of life and death in this connection would depend largely on how harsh the forthcoming winters would prove to be. One fact must be remembered above all others. Merlins and the species on which they preyed had coexisted through countless aeons of time.

Thoughts turned to 1973 and what it might have in store.

THE THIRD YEAR

11
The Search

In 1973, spring came late to the moor. On 19 April the hawthorns in the upland valley were barely in bud. On the plucking post, careful searching brought to light nothing except a few faded feathers from 1972 kills.

Several pairs of songbirds had staked out territories towards the head of the valley. A cock wheatear displayed on a rock just above where I sat sheltering from the chill breeze; a pair of ring ousels excavated for worms in the turf. 'Excavated' is the right word. Not for them the cautious probing of their cousin the blackbird. The bill was used like a pick-axe, spoil flying in all directions.

A little after midday an unusually large and handsomely coloured buzzard hunted the valley, quartering the ground a few feet up more in the manner of a harrier than its own species. Buteo concluded the performance by perching on the very branch where first we had seen the hen merlin at rest in 1972. It could hardly have hit upon an apter way of demonstrating that the merlins had not yet returned to the valley. As I stood up to go, the first pair of collared doves I had ever seen there flew in and landed in one of the bare thorns. Walking back along the moorland track, I heard a familiar fluting whistle. A pair of golden plover ran, froze, ran again, flew. Another species not seen before on that moor. It being late April, one might reasonably hope that they would remain to breed.

I did not revisit the moor until 8 May. Still, spring hung back; the moor bleak and almost deserted. Fewer curlews, fewer lapwings. Not even the usual number of meadow pipits were in evidence along the track up to the valley.

Halfway up, we stopped to watch a hen kestrel hovering low. Another bird appeared, flying just above the lifeless heather directly towards us. Turning slightly as she drew level, she passed 4ft up and an arm's length away, every feather clearly distinguishable. A hen merlin; pale enough to be the same bird we had watched last year, but alone, as far as we could see. Nevertheless, our journey was completed with quickened step and mounting enthusiasm.

An hour's watching in the valley brought sightings of pipits, ring ousels, high-flying snipe. The cock wheatear seen on 19 April was missing, but his feathers were not in evidence on the plucking post – nor any others.

A shallower, less rocky valley lay a mile away over the moor, bounded by a gently sloping hillside studded with well-grown hawthorns. It was one of the places where we had watched for merlins in previous years. Thither we made our way; to find the 'man on the spot' already engaged in investigation. We joined forces and together put up the biggest number of snipe either of us had ever seen anywhere on the moor. Wherever moisture had collected in a hollow, a pair were in residence: but we failed to flush a merlin. We had drawn a blank.

My friend had during the previous week received reports of a merlin seen in several places on the moor, but always a solitary female. It began to look as though the handsome male had failed to survive the winter. After all, it is the cocks which arrive on the breeding territories first; or so the theory goes. Not that the winter had been a hard one, but the estuaries where merlins winter in South Wales are in many places infested by wildfowlers of the 'marsh cowboy' order who destroy a number of rare and protected birds by their unfortunate practice of shooting first and asking questions afterwards.

During the rest of May we kept in regular contact. Sightings were reported, including one of a cock, but never in circumstances which suggested where a nest might be. One thing alone was clear; that the crows' nest site used in 1972 was not in use in 1973. At the end of May, I carried out a methodical and comprehensive search of every part of the moor not already covered. There were golden plover on the high tops and some were certainly breeding. So the operation yielded some information . . . but none of merlins – not so much as a single

Agility on the wing is of prime importance. A hen merlin checks her impetus in order to turn sharply, as she would in pursuit of a meadow pipit *(Dennis Green)*

Typical landscape in merlin country. The 'mawn' pool shown (old peat-cuttings) is the actual site of the incident described on page 25 *(H. McSweeney)*

The head of a typical nesting dingle. One of the trees in the picture has already been used by crows as a site for their nest which merlins may eventually occupy
(*H. McSweeney*)

A hunt that failed. A hen merlin applies the airbrakes prior to resuming occupation of her observation post on a tall spray of heather *(Dennis Green)*

sighting. Not even one pile of pipit feathers lay on any of the possible plucking posts visited, despite the investigation of every known hummock on twenty square miles of heather-clad hills. The suspicion could no longer be escaped that the reported sighting of a cock merlin was probably a case of mistaken identity and that the hen, having waited on the moor for some weeks in vain, had moved on north. That, it seemed, was that.

June passed uneventfully, attention turned to less spectacular birds nearer home. As we sat down to dinner on the evening of 1 July, the phone rang. I picked up the receiver. 'Mr Orton?' said an eager young voice. 'I've been watching a hen merlin and a hobby fighting over a valley. I saw the cock merlin too. He perched in a tree for nearly half an hour . . . I'll tell you exactly where from the Ordnance Survey sheet.'

12
The Find

The area lay well to the north of the valley in Radnorshire; on a different map, in fact. So these merlins could not have been last year's birds on a new site.

The hobby was a real surprise. One knew that odd pairs bred north of their strongholds south of the Thames, but a hobby in this district offered nutritious food for thought.

Urgently, I fished on the bookshelf for the appropriate OS sheet. The valley was soon found. From the pattern of the water courses seaming it, so was the exact spot where the intriguing observations had been made. Or so I thought. It was a big valley, in a major hill formation: not so very secluded, and accessible by public right of way. But access was not easy, involving a steep climb followed by rough walking across broken and boggy terrain.

But it was a magnificent valley, with luxuriant heather, not much bracken and acres of dense bilberry. Much larger in all dimensions than the area watched in 1972, such intimacy with the merlins might not be repeated, but there should not be the frustration of birds vanishing over an all-too-proximate skyline within seconds of a sighting. Here, once the binoculars were on a merlin, it should be possible to keep it in view for some time and thereby learn that much more of what went on. Always supposing, of course, that there really was a breeding pair in residence.

There were outcrops of rock, some tall enough to merit the term cliff, and many trees. Thorns, ashes and rowans clothed the steep shoulders; there were even substantial oaks dotted here and there. Alders, too, grew in the valley bottom, contributing to an altogether richer habitat; a habitat that, on the face of it, possessed every amenity a merlin could desire. 5 July was the date of this first visit.

I studied the map again. The folds in the hills, the stream beds, the exact positions of groups of trees and bushes. Yes: I was in the right place; no doubt of it. Those thorns down below must be where the cock merlin perched; that shoulder over yonder the scene of the fight between the falcons. The day wore on, growing hotter. Flies were a torment. A kestrel with plumage in rags came to hunt over the crest immediately behind me. Was she moulting half her main feathers at once? Hardly likely. Was she, perhaps, the victim of some parasitic infestation? Or a hen which had brooded eggs and nestlings in a taken-over nest too small for her? Kestrels sometimes do this. There was one in Radnorshire which had tried to rear four young in a woodpigeon's nest. A friend had brought himself, he believed, within inches of a coronary rescuing the young from the public highway day after day and carrying them back to the nest 200ft up a one in four hillside.

A second kestrel ascended. Also with damaged – but less damaged – plumage. Then a young cock sparrowhawk circled up from immediately below. Down at the mouth of the valley, just in sight, were extensive oak woods. Over them sailed a pair of buzzards. Hawks in plenty, but where were the merlins? Hawks in plenty: *birds* in plenty. Many redstarts in the trees below; the upper air alive with swifts and swallows. Every second heather clump the haunt of pipit or whinchat. Woodpigeons murmured; flapped heavily from tree to tree. Four kestrels now hung over the skyline; a buzzard carrying a mole laboured through the overheated air. But no merlins.

At 2.00 pm, I came to the conclusion that no merlin resided in that valley. My young friend had enjoyed a stroke of luck. The day of his visit, attracted there after all by nothing more than intriguing features glimpsed on a map, a pair of non-breeders had happened to pass through. So I had half suspected from the beginning.

These reflections were interrupted by a dark brown bird flying up the hillside 30yd to my left, moving fast on swiftly beaten wings. Fairly long wings, tapering sharply from shoulders a little broader than a kestrel's. Wrenching myself round, I got the glasses on just as she passed over the skyline. An undeniable hen merlin, although exceptionally dark in her upper plumage.

Following falcons on foot in the hope of a further sighting is among the more forlorn of human prospects. But, fortunately, we rarely learn from past disappointments. Up I went, puffing and grunting, to reach the crest a few minutes later. No second sighting of the hen: but the cock got up from underfoot and flew 30yd before vanishing into dead ground. The binoculars showed him to be coloured the dullest of pale slate above, little brighter than a kestrel below – very different from last year's bird. In one other particular he differed, too. He had intermediate barring on his tail, which, as the story goes on, becomes a matter of some significance.

I continued to follow, but apart from the briefest glimpse of one or other of the merlins flashing back across the skyline we had all recently crossed, the effort was unrewarded.

Because I stupidly failed to note landmarks as I laboured up to the crest, I mislaid my OP, situated as it was in the repetitive pattern of heather, bracken and bilberry which characterised the hillside. Left at the OP were several useful items of personal property, so it had to be rediscovered. Hardly the day and circumstances for half an hour's additional scrambling up and down a steep slope, but necessity knows no laws. At last I found the OP, accompanied there by several hundred flies disturbed as I blundered through the bracken.

At 4.45 a bird, taken at first for just another kestrel, approached from up-valley at a little above eye level. Wearily, the heavy binoculars were riased and focused. The 'kestrel' was a cock merlin flying with leisurely wing beats, another unusual specimen in several respects. Seen at this angle, wings and tail looked to be exceptionally long; again, the colour, both above and below, looked very dull. But the bird was unquestionably a merlin. The buff sides and back to the neck were plain as a pikestaff; also the absence of the facial mask which a hobby would have displayed clearly at that distance.

What *had* my young friend really seen? Cock and hen merlin

in mock combat? He had said that the perched cock merlin had not been noticed until after the fight. His knowledge of birds and the accuracy of his observation were exceptionally reliable, but circumstantial evidence had begun to mount against the hobby. One thing I had been unable to see as the merlin went by was whether the original impression of intermediate tail bars could be confirmed.

And so back home, with food for thought.

My young friend reacted to my phone call with surprising news. I had not been in the right place in the valley; I had been wrong by a mile. Oddly enough, the pattern of vegetation and water courses was virtually duplicated in another place much nearer the head of the valley. The right place.

The next day was Saturday; he was free to join and guide us. We arrived at 10.10 am, the weather fine, dry and breezy – conditions infinitely to be preferred to the intense heat of the 5th. The breeze kept the flies down; this time, a sufficiency of liquid refreshment was carried, despite the weight.

Striding on past my first OP, we arrived at an outcrop of rock overlooking a part of the valley which our guide recognised without difficulty. Before we had time to settle down, the hen merlin flew along the valley bottom, circled, and perched in a half-dead oak, riven by lightning, with half its branches lichened and sprawling near the ground. She and the cock had both been put up unintentionally by a curlew engaged in mobbing a crow. The cock had flown we knew not where; all binoculars, as it so happened, being trained at the time on the hen. For half an hour she remained in the tree, then took off and vanished. Our distance from the birds was considerable; it seemed that it might be reduced to some extent without disturbing them. This we did. From the new OP, some of the stream bed was out of sight; but merlins, if seen again at all, would be seen to much better advantage.

For half an hour nothing happened. Then the hen merlin flew into view, screaming. She buzzed the ground, leading us straight to where the cock stood in the shadow thrown by a

small thorn bush. She continued along the hillside, still screaming. The cock took off, circled to gain height, crossed the skyline. His mate followed close behind. Still, her screams echoed
round the valley. What were we to make of it? Belated and aber-
rant courtship behaviour on the part of birds organically
damaged and mentally deranged by organochlorine pesticide
residues? It seemed all too probable.

The merlins came and went throughout the early afternoon;
the behaviour already described was typical of what followed.
But at 4.00 I saw a bird – taken at first for a hen kestrel – vanish
into a big oak: the biggest and most densely foliaged tree on the
hillside. Obscured as they were by the vegetation, I caught only
the sketchiest glimpses of the bird's movements which took it,
stage by stage, to the thickest foliage of all up near the crown.
As the breeze stirred the leaves, the jumble of sticks and twigs
from which the carrion crow weaves its nest could just be made
out. Now, the bird was in a less dense patch of foliage and could
be seen distinctly enough for it to be apparent that she was
bending forward as though tending nestlings. There came the
unmistakeable squeeping of young hawks. The adult bird left
the tree, revealing herself as the hen merlin. She flew from perch
to perch, calling. Scrutinising the tree with extra care, I found a
concentration of droppings on the ground directly below the
dense patch of foliage up in the crown. We had discovered
another merlins' nest. In a tree again; and in another area of
abundant and suitable heather. Eventually, the hen flew from
view.

Half an hour later, there came an announcement from my
companion, then scanning the ridge above and behind us. 'I've
got her again, up over the crest – look!'

I was already looking in the same direction, at the kestrel
with the ragged plumage, which we had by now named 'Tatty'.
'No, it isn't,' I replied.

'It's the hobby!' cried my wife and young friend in unison.

I lowered the glasses in order to wither my companions with
a glance. But two birds soared over the crest; one leaden dark
with the scimitar wings of a swift. It shrugged them in to hold its

station in a gust of wind which would otherwise have carried it 50ft higher than it wished to be. The hastily refocused binoculars revealed dark eyes staring down from a bandit's black mask: a darkly streaked breast, tibials tinged russet.

The appearance was brief, the impact lasting. When the merlins returned, their glamour was slightly dimmed. The hen flew in calling, visited the tree where we believed the nest to be. Among the decaying branches of a small dead thorn close by, the cock sat preening. There he continued to sit, preening and dozing by turns, for the hour which remained before our departure.

13

Out into the World

At last, after three months of frustration, the iron glowed hot. Much had been missed by the find having been made so late in the season, but much of interest might still be learned.

On 10 July I was back, two days after the previous visit. A different and less arduous approach had been found, at the expense of traversing a few extra acres of wetland. Snipe and curlew abounded. As the ground dried out and bog plants gave way to heather, coveys of grouse erupted from the path. The young were at all stages of development, from cheepers to birds three-quarters grown.

After just fifteen minutes on an OP somewhat lower down the slope, screaming was heard and the 'tyuk tyuk' call associated with the presentation of food. There was movement behind the dense foliage of the big oak; movement by more than one bird. When the cock merlin flew out the noise subsided. Evidently a food presentation – by the cock, directly. This confirmed what the calendar indicated; that the young must be well advanced.

An hour later, the hen flew in calling, circled the valley at high speed, flew out again without visiting the nest. Ten minutes after she had gone, there was fresh movement behind the screen of foliage and a nestling clambered out to perch on a high twig and survey the world it was shortly to inherit. It looked plump, confident and healthy. After last year's experience, I held my breath. But a stout oak makes a better gymnasium than a dense and tangled hawthorn does.

After half an hour spent chiefly in plucking down from its plumage and watching it float away on the breeze with evident interest, the young merlin went back indoors. Pigeons and piston aircraft had passed overhead. All had been watched attentively until out of sight: none so far as could be seen had inspired fear or even caution. The time was now 2.10 pm. At 2.25 the hen came to the valley, again circling noisily without landing. At 2.35 the hobby passed directly overhead, flying fast. At 2.45, the hen merlin returned for the third time. Falling from the sky like a thunderbolt, she circled the nest tree screaming, but again without entering.

The suspicion that I was now *persona non grata* could not be avoided. There were reasons for a brief return to the car, an oversight in the matter of notebook and pencil among them. Having assembled jacket, vacuum flask, binocular case and knapsack to form a neat and plainly unabandoned pile by a rock, I left. The walk to and from the car took an hour. My return was greeted with merlin noise coming from several places at once. The hen was in flight, going down-valley. Young birds were squeeping and wing-exercising behind the foliage. The most strident calls came from closer at hand. The profile of the hillside above the OP was convex; the slope clad in dense heather and bilberry. From where I stood, the OP was not visible. Half expecting that something of interest was about to happen, I picked my way down with caution and stealth. Edging forward, I could just see the rocks. Lying there, exactly as they had been left, were rolled jacket, flask, binocular case and knapsack. Gazing down at them from the rock by which they lay was the cock merlin. Mutual discovery was instantaneous and he was off in a flash, chattering angrily. Collecting my property, I withdrew to another outcrop of rock 200yd farther away.

The calling continued, but for some minutes no bird was seen. Then the hen rose above the skyline on the far side of the valley. As I spotted her, she stooped; directing attention to her mate, already perched up there on a heather clump. She alighted beside him: he immediately took off. Eight woodpigeons were strung out in extended line, feeding among the bilberries and occupying a hundred yards of hillside. All were buzzed and put up, with a hint of anger in the attacks. The motivation may have been the release of aggressions aroused by our sudden confrontation on the merlin's territory, a release which appeared to stimulate appetite. A patch of gorse stood right on the skyline. At this the merlin stooped again and again, presumably to flush some small bird he knew to be there. After each stoop he flung up to hang 20ft above and 10ft downwind of the gorse. The retreat of any bird seeking an escape route downwind was thus cut off while the merlin was poised to stoop into the wind under perfect control if his prey made the mistake of trying to leave by the front door. The prey knew better than to emerge from the sanctuary of the gorse on any terms, and the merlin's final stoop was directed at his mate. One touch of nature makes the whole world kin.

He flew to a perch on a post which had once formed part of a fence long since collapsed in decay. A pipit was whirled along the ridge by the gusty wind, high above the merlin. Leaving his post, he climbed to the attack, but the pipit rose faster. The merlin, acknowledging his limitations, wasted neither time nor effort in fruitless pursuit. All hawks show reluctance to tackle prey already airborne and above them, a rule to which there are few exceptions. Returning to his post, the merlin preened methodically. Fifteen minutes later he left; crossing the far skyline with the hen in line astern. Redirecting my attention to the oak, I found the enterprising youngster out again, still busily de-downing his plumage. A sibling – or more than one – called from the nest, where energetically beaten wings could be seen through the foliage. Thus passed the rest of the afternoon.

At 6.00 the hen came over the far skyline to land in a sparse thorn tossed violently to and fro by a wind now risen from fresh to gale-force. She found difficulty in perching comfortably and nearly lost her footing when one of a pair of passing woodpigeons clumsily buzzed her. There was no immediate retaliation. Instead, she allowed the pigeons to settle down to feed among the bilberries, watching them intently. Having given them sufficient time to relax the special caution most birds display on arriving anywhere, she gathered herself, dropped silently from the tree and attacked low. One pigeon fled, the other collapsed sprawling on the ground. The merlin flew away over the horizon. It is often difficult to believe that merlins do not possess a sense of humour. Eventually, the pigeon recovered from its shock and followed its companion.

At 6.15 the young merlin went back inside: tyuk-tyukking followed. The cock fell in a stoop from the tree and flew away along the valley bottom. The ensuing silence suggested that his visit had not been without its practical aspect.

Half an hour later, the youngster was in view again; but when I left at 7.15 he had retired, possibly for the night.

The next visit was on 12 July. The weather was cloudy and humid, what breeze there was blew from the north-west. At 11.00 a young merlin sat out on the branch; another exercised its wings half in view. Twenty minutes later it emerged to sit beside its sibling. It was bigger, paler, plumper. Much more down adhered to its feathers, particularly on its rump. They 'kissed' as budgerigars kiss, plucked down in unison; then, briefly, plucked down from each other. A snowstorm of the stuff drifted away on the breeze.

At 11.27, a solitary mistlethrush alighted near them in the tree, made a mobbing pass at the fledglings, but more as a gesture than with evidently dire intent. The merlins ignored it entirely. More mistlethrushes touched down, calling their harsh hawk-baiting cry. Nine, ten, eventually fourteen; and a young blackbird, bereft of its few wits by the example of all that brave company. Gathering courage – an attribute with which the mistlethrush is generously endowed – they pressed closer. Soon, all were packed into the crown of the tree. The infant merlins were beset on all sides. I grew anxious, knowing something of mistlethrush mobbing-potential from past experience. Once, I had seen a marauding tomcat, the terror of the neighbourhood, demoralised into ignominious flight by a mere pair of these formidable birds. But such fears were groundless. The senior fledgling, fixing the nearest thrush with an unwinking stare, raised a foot; clenched it; opened it; clenched it again slowly. The mistlethrushes fell silent. All became preoccupied with caterpillars – real or imaginary – among the twigs of the oak. One by one, unhurriedly, they withdrew. It may be that the urge to save face is not an exclusively human foible. Preening was resumed; but by noon both young merlins squeeped incessantly, from hunger, or so we presumed.

The hobby flew up-valley, low along the crest of the opposite hillside, over which it eventually vanished. At 12.43 pm it reappeared; flying a reciprocal course with a small bird dangling from one foot. At 12.55 a sixth sense made me look round in time to duck an attempt by an immature but extremely handsome young kestrel to remove my head from my shoulders. Flying between us, it passed on down the slope to perch in a tree in the valley bottom, all participants in the drama displaying symptoms of surprise. The young merlins, the marginal nature of its seniority notwithstanding, then importuned the young kestrel for food. Eventually, it escaped their attentions by flying to join Tatty and her mate in the sky. From the amiable reception accorded to it, we presumed it to be a member of the family.

The three kestrels played on in the sky together: the hobby again flew along the ridge, obviously hunting. Whether one hobby or two visited the valley, the conviction grew that hunting on this scale must imply hungry nestlings somewhere. Bird-hawks do not hunt at hourly intervals to satisfy merely their own appetites.

A strange kestrel perched on a skyline fence post. A cock wheatear buzzed it, the kestrel retreated, the wheatear occupied the post to wheeze a song of triumph. Distracted by this episode, we missed the arrival of the cock merlin, signalled by an outburst of noise from the youngsters. Food was delivered. We saw him leave, via a perch in a tall thorn where he sat for some minutes, facing us with one foot drawn up in a stance of singular elegance, as though posing for a photograph. Very smart he looked in the clear light, despite his comparatively drab colouring. When he left, a party of mistlethrushes pursued him; but not too energetically.

A little after 2.00 the hobby put in another appearance. With but a single food delivery, followed so quickly by silence, it seemed likely that the prey had been shared. If last year's pattern was to be repeated, a point in time would arrive in the development of the young when this would no longer happen. When, we wondered? For a drowsy hour, silence reigned supreme.

From where we sat, the view of the nest and its immediate surroundings was good; of the whole shoulder, for that matter. But the extensive moorland we knew to lie beyond the crest lay also beyond our view. And it was in that direction that the hobby had gone after all but one of its visits. We could remain where we sat and keep the young merlins under continuous observation, or we could withdraw to a higher vantage point from which more of the hobby's hunting terrain could be seen. The lie of the land was such that the second option would mean losing sight of the big oak entirely; but that was the choice we made. The decision was rewarded within minutes. First by the entrancing sight of a young kestrel in pursuit of a cabbage butterfly, compelled by the dancing flight of the insect to display its utmost agilities; then by the return of the hobby.

As we had hoped, the arena was in full view. The dark falcon came from down-valley, long flickering wings driving it at high speed. It flew on a course closing in on us gradually, but it turned away as it drew level to quarter the moor methodically, working its way upwind until level with the head of the valley. Then it rose swiftly, clawing up in tight spirals towards the hirundines fly-hawking in the upper air. Suddenly, it was among them: then rising through them. A mocking pass at one swift; a vicious closed-wing stoop at a second – very narrowly evaded. A feint was then made at a third, a change of direction almost too fast for the eye to follow and an incredible climbing attack on a fourth target which culminated in the hobby flicking over on its back to snatch with one foot at the unwary bird only inches above it. But the air was moist and heavy, the advantage with the swifts. Discouraged, the hobby circled on up until lost in the haze.

Half an hour later, the bird – or its mate – came again; patient low-level pipit-hunting resumed. Once more the cock merlin brought food to his young. At 6.00 we departed.

14

Flight

A weekend fell on 14–15 July. Arranging an overnight stop in the district, we planned to devote the whole of it to the merlins, weather permitting. The forecast was not encouraging, but the 14th dawned fair enough for us to be on the OP quite early.

Within five minutes the male fledgling flew from the oak to a line of rocks 30yd away. My forecast had been that he would fly on the 16th. He had beaten it by two days.

There was no sign of the other youngster, in the tree or elsewhere. Nor in the next two hours, during which there was a sharp shower of rain. Anxiety grew. Had she, before our arrival, been lured out prematurely by the precocious venturesomeness of her brother? And come to grief thereby? Her remains were nowhere in evidence on the hillside. But were they likely to be? A fox, for example, would probably have carried her to its earth.

During those two hours the young cock had flown freely, sampling perches on rocks, on heather clumps, in bushes and quite high in the trees. His performance improved with every flight; his rate of climb seemed sufficient to take him quickly into a tree top if danger were to threaten. The misgivings we had felt on his account diminished, stubby tail and abbreviated primaries notwithstanding. But fears for his sister's welfare were not quieted until, as the rain ceased, there came an outburst of calling followed by her appearance in the top of the oak. There she remained alone for an hour, at the end of which time her brother made his longest flight yet to join her. Ten minutes later, their father visited the nest, but if he brought food their reaction was strangely muted. Having spent several minutes out of sight in the tree with the fledglings, he flew out, via perches in several different trees, to cross the skyline with a mobbing curlew in attendance.

A bare fifteen minutes later he returned, but again it was impossible to see whether prey was delivered. This time, on leaving the nest he flew straight to the ridge and vanished over it. Immediately after, the young resumed calling and a merlin was seen flying along the skyline. It was the hen. She flew to the small windswept thorn high on the hillside, which had been the scene of her passage of arms with the pigeons a few days earlier. The male fledgling flew to the rocks nearest to the nest tree; his sister perched in view in its crown. For half an hour, all three merlins sat frozen in their postures, like heraldic symbols blazoned on an escutcheon.

Eventually, the hen took off and flew straight to the oak, dropping immediately to the nest. Although partly obscured by foliage, it was soon apparent that she fed, tearing at prey held down by one foot. As nothing had been carried to the nest by her, it followed that she fed from a kill brought by the cock but left unconsumed by the fledglings. Since little had been brought in since our arrival, successful activity earlier in the morning was implied. Extra effort inspired by precognition of worsening weather? Perhaps.

Her hunger satisfied, the hen flew from the tree carrying the remnant left after her meal for presentation to her son on the rocks, who now accepted and fed from it voraciously. The hen then quitted the valley, but was soon back, bearing a fresh kill. This, too, was surrendered to the young cock who fed from it with an appetite not visibly diminished.

The fledglings stood side by side, sharing the kill. The hen flew to a perch 150yd away where she remained for some time. After the meal, the young male dropped to the ground, scratching about as though trying to take a dust bath. Afterwards, he settled down to roost in the posture of a domestic hen. With head tucked into scapularies, he dozed off: where prowling fox, stoat or weasel could leap on him before he had the least inkling of its approach. The hen moved another 50yd farther away, her daughter perched in the very top of the oak, wing-exercising with vigour.

Her first adventure into flight could not be long delayed. On reflection, two things struck me. One, that the hen, so noisy until the 12th, had been silent all day; the other that we had been privileged to enjoy an unprecedented amount of her company. Since the 12th, the wind had gone round through 180° so that the hillside was now sheltered from it. That, we assumed, accounted for the change.

Walking back to the car, it came as no surprise to see the hobby – missing from the scene all day – pipit-hunting on the moor up behind where we had been sitting. It had, no doubt, passed to and fro out of sight behind us several times during the day. Raptors are extremely sensitive to the wind, the pattern of their behaviour responding to changes in its force and direction.

The hobby flew low and fast, almost black in the poor light which percolated through dense grey clouds covering the whole sky but piled up ominously dark on the eastern horizon. Rain coming into the Welsh Marches in mid-July on an *east* wind: the situation was unusual, to say the least of it. I felt uneasy.

Rain fell heavily during the night. The following morning, the hill tops were capped in murky haze, the air saturated. Although it was not yet actually raining, it could be only a matter of time. If we were allowed a few hours of uninterrupted watching, we might count ourselves lucky.

Between the track where I usually left the car and the merlins' valley mist lay thick – thicker than I had realised when I set out without a compass. An hour later, with not a landmark in sight, I was lost. Carefully, I reconstructed in my mind the route followed, allowing for the fact that, blinded by mist, we were bound instinctively to have walked in a circle. I had led. Which of my two legs was the dominant limb? The left. So we had very probably circled to the right, as my left leg automatically took a pace a fraction of an inch longer than the right; a fault one corrects unconsciously by reference to landmarks when one can see where one is going. If that assumption was correct, a broad and unfamiliar track which had just loomed up out of the mist was unfamiliar no longer;

but it meant we had indeed circled far to the right. Using it as a provisional landmark, I set a fresh course through the now thinning mist. The guess had been a good one. In visibility which improved minute by minute, we made a bee-line for the OP.

Forty minutes later, we were there; just as the great banks of mist rolled away entirely to admit weak sunshine into the valley from a sky still pregnant with threat. The wind continued to blow from the east. For the first half-hour after our belated arrival, nothing at all happened. Then two homing pigeons flew along the ridge opposite. One was rather like a stock dove, the other an extraordinary bird coloured not unlike a French partridge. What on earth was it? Something nagged away in the back of my mind, then burst forward into conscious recollection. A 'scanderoon', for heaven's sake! It was only in June that I had made the acquaintance of the variety from reading Henry Williamson's book of the same name.

Mistlethrushes entered the valley, churring. At noon there was merlin noise, but the birds could not be found. Fifteen minutes later, both fledglings were seen flying along the shoulder towards the oak. They passed it to alight sprawling on the ground beyond, under the knotted branches of a small tree long dead and far gone in decay. Around the twisted bole of this tree the female pursued her brother on foot; both waddling and stumbling clumsily on the rough and broken ground. Grounded hawks, unless motionless, lose all dignity. The young male probed and scratched at the roots of the tree. A mouse broke from cover and scampered down the slope. Both young merlins galloped after it, reptiles again, forgetful of their wings. Predictably, the mouse escaped.

One young merlin hopped up on the stump of a fallen tree, the other flew to the top of the oak riven to semi-ruin by lightning of long ago. Soon the former took off, after struggling successfully to overcome the difficulties imposed by the lack of breeze and a cluttered runway. It flew to the long line of rocks to preen.

At 1.15, there now being a likelihood that rain would hold off for an hour or two longer, I walked back to the car accompanied by one other member of the small party with me that day, to fetch the picnic lunch left there in expectations of our being driven off by the rain well before the morning had ended. On the way back, when within a few minutes' walk of the OP, a long-winged dark bird came up out of the heather 5yd away. The silhouette said 'kestrel'; the colour 'hobby'. Yet there was a hint of sparrowhawk, too. This series of false impressions raced in succession through my mind, all, perhaps, within a fraction of a second. 20yd away, the bird turned, hung in the air for a brief moment, then dropped to a perch on a heather clump. The glasses established its identity immediately. A cuckoo. I was reminded of an absent friend, a good ornithologist. When handed a dead bird for identification one day, he scratched his head in uncertainty. Suddenly, his face lit up with inspiration. Marching to a nearby fence, he balanced the bird's body on a rail. Striding 30yd away, he turned, drew binoculars from their case as a duellist might draw pistol, focused . . . and identified the bird unerringly.

Back at the OP, we found that the young merlins had been kept under observation as they flew hither and thither sampling many attractive perches. The pattern of 1972 was repeated; neither bird could rest content for long if the other was not near, or at least in view, except on occasions when some large and succulent insect had just been caught in the heather. Then, the priority would be on privacy, so that the prey might be consumed in peace.

Eventually, the cock arrived, with a bright whinchat in his talons. The young were together on the rocks at the time. The kill was dropped at their feet to become the object of a noisy tug-of-war. The young male won and fled with his prize, his sister in raucous pursuit. She followed him to the ground to challenge possession again. Each squared up to the other, big brother proving victorious. On the previous day, a kill had been shared. On this showing, it looked as though emergence of all nestlings might trigger a hostile refusal to share. One rule for the nest: another for the outside world. It made sense.

At 4.30, thunder pealed. I took a serious look at the sky – the first for half an hour – then caught the eye of the only other male member of the party. In seconds, we were packed up, the binoculars safely cased, and *en route* for the car. We made it with a minute to spare before the heavens opened.

Rain usually approaches these hills from a westerly direction, the full fury of the storms already spent over the higher formations which lie in serried ranks for most of the way to the coast. With the rain clouds coming in from the east, across the wide North Midland plain, they were almost the first range of hills to confront the depression. So, in these conditions, they would have to take the full initial force of the storm. They certainly did. The drainage systems, both natural and man-made, were far from equal to what they had to cope with and within an hour the roads were axle-deep in flood water.

Merlins, we had learned in 1972, resisted the wet very well; but what of hobbies? It is widely held that the factor confining the British population so largely to the counties south and east of the source of the Thames is rainfall. The hobby is a dry-weather species; its nestlings highly vulnerable to a wetting. Hobbies are excellent mothers, instinctively aware of this and of their duty to use their own wings and bodies to provide extra shelter in a storm. But there are storms and storms. Rain had poured down during the night. Now it fell in sheets; some of the heaviest rain I had ever encountered in England or Wales at any time of the year. The sort of rain which eventually reduces the feathers of any terrestrial bird to a sodden ruin. By now, the out-stretched wings of the hen hobby would be plastered flat, breached. Cold rain might be driving through them, dripping fatally on nestlings still in down.

The sky grew even darker; the rain colder and yet heavier. Prudently, as it transpired, I re-routed the car home to avoid all low-lying river crossings.

The rain continued without remission until dawn.

15

Expanding Activities

On the 18th, the question uppermost in mind was the fate of any hobby nestlings there may have been before the downpour.

The wind was now back in the south-west, and although the sky was far from clear the cloud was high, the feel of the air comparatively dry. But watercourses which had been dry ran full; patches of previously negotiable bog were passable no longer. The route we had to take across the moor was hardly more direct than that taken inadvertently in the fog. So we did not arrive at our destination until well into the morning.

Kestrels hovered over the ridges on both sides of the valley, a curlew flew and called incessantly with an unfamiliar cry. Not the 'koorli koorli' call: nor the trill. It was a repeated 'che-che-che-che-chew', reminiscent of other waders. If I had heard it before, I had certainly not associated the sound with its authentic source.

On the 12th, a young kestrel, flying down the hillside from behind, had narrowly avoided colliding with me. The hobby now did likewise, pulling away with creaking wings less than a yard overhead. Thus twice in seven days did I escape decapitation in a highly original form! The view of the bird was the best so far; especially so as it checked boldly in front of us to hang on the wind for a moment or two as it scrutinised this new and doubtless unwelcome obstruction placed in a hard-working hunter's flight path. This was encouraging. All things being equal, raptors hunting for themselves alone are usually on the prowl soon after sunrise. Should they need to hunt twice in the day, the second period of activity takes place between mid-afternoon and last light. A hobby on the move during the late morning implied that there were still nestlings to be fed, so the effects of the deluge may not have been so lethal after all.

Evidence of merlins was there none. By 12.30, concluding

that the valley had been deserted, we withdrew to the higher OP from which the wide vistas beyond the far ridge came into view. But we had guessed wrong. Half an hour later, a party of ramblers appeared, making their way up the course of the stream. As they came nearer, they passed from view under the bulge of the hillside. By judging the speed of their progress, it was possible to assess accurately their arrival in the critical area although they could no longer be seen. Merlin-protest, prolonged and vociferous, confirmed our judgement. But from where we sat, the birds were not seen. Should we move downhill again? It seemed logical to do so now that the birds had declared themselves present, so we did.

They were not on view: but the hobby appeared immediately, rising above and falling below the skyline as it hunted the moor which we had had under observation ten minutes earlier. There was no doubt about it. It was shaping up to be 'one of those days'.

Kestrels dominated the scene, Tatty and her mate included. He, too, showed quill damage but in less extreme form. The curlews laboured to dominate the kestrels, mobbing fiercely when their favourite feeding ground, a broad marshy patch of ground high on the opposite shoulder, was overflown.

There was not a glimpse of a merlin until 2.45, when scanning the shoulder for the umpteenth time revealed one perched high in the lightning-riven tree. Within a few minutes it flew, first to a rock beside a trickle of water threading the curlews' feeding ground, then along the hillside to flop down in the bracken. Ten minutes later both were on the wing, displaying flight and tail quills grown to adult length. All this was in less than 72 hours. White tips to the tail feathers, absent from the well-worn plumage of the adult hen, showed clearly. Later on, this was to become an important distinguishing feature. While the various slight differences in appearance between juveniles and their mother can be seen plainly enough when the birds are together, it is another matter when an isolated bird is seen, especially when the light is inadequate.

The birds perched for five minutes, then took off again, flying in evident excitement from perch to perch. The cock appeared, following a course which brought him past us, then away over the ridge behind. Searching again for the juveniles, we found one in a tree with a magpie shaping up to mob it. The merlin flew to its sibling (which youngster was which we had failed to detect in the confusion of movement) but the invitation to commune was rejected. For good reason. Juvenile Number 2 was mantling the kill delivered by its father before we had seen him. It flew with its prey to a jumble of boulders 300yd from the oak; the longest flight we had yet witnessed. The other flew to the nearer rocks where a meadow pipit fluttered over its head, twittering. The young merlin ignored it. Was this because it was crop-full, or had the bird-hunting instinct still to develop? Was it wholly an instinct – or was it partly a taught skill? Perhaps we should discover.

The magpie, which had made no attempt to pursue either merlin, flew now to the back of a sheep grazing among the bracken. This it searched for vermin, specially round the root of the tail, uttering soft high-pitched croaks as it did so. One might almost use the word 'coo'. Was this reassurance to calm the beast? The sounds certainly bore a remarkable resemblance to those made for that purpose by human beings when tending nervous livestock.

As the afternoon passed, the merlins flew frequently, still showing a strong disposition to enjoy each others' company but passionate reunions were no longer the order of the day. Emotional development, it appeared, was as rapid as quill growth. One flight ended with the young male grounded amidst bracken and boulders right under a thorn with branches sweeping so low that a Christmas tree was called to mind. Up into this he wished to fly, but three attempts failed to raise him from the ground. Finally, the problem was solved by legs flexed so sharply that his breast touched the ground, a great thrusting leap and a mighty flailing of wings.

Food was delivered by the cock at 4.00 and again at 5.30. At 5.45 shortly after his daughter had left a perch on the ground to fly purposefully to the lightning-riven tree, the cock was seen leaving it. He first circled towards us, then zig-zagged up the opposite slope, working his way towards the spur which bounded the shoulder as one looked down-valley. Passing over this just high enough to be seen against a background of sky, he closed his wings and fell in a stoop at something out of sight beyond the spur. Three minutes later, noise in the riven tree drew our attention to him as he left it yet again. There was little doubt that he had made four kills in the space of $1\frac{3}{4}$ hours, one unusually near the nest site.

The last hour was uneventful. At no time during an eight-hour day had we seen the hen. The more closely one watched merlins, the more there seemed to be which one might have in common with them.

Holidays, too, perhaps!

On 21 July the wind blew freshly from the west, cloud rolled along the higher ridges. In the valley, though, visibility was adequate.

We arrived to see a brown merlin depart in a hurry. As it flew beyond the spur and away, our conclusion that it was the adult hen was confirmed by the youngsters beginning to call. Within a few minutes they were up over the crest, riding the gusts to practise 'fighter tactics'. As with the 1972 birds, their fluency on the wing a mere seven days after leaving the nest was astonishing. Astonishing, that is to say, by the standards of an animal which takes at least 20 per cent of its allotted span to reach an equivalent level of development. The game continued for some time, as every attempt by either bird to land in a tree-top for a breather was met by the other with persistent buzzing until the challenge was accepted and the combat resumed.

At 12.10, there may have been a presentation. If so, it was missed due to spitting rain which by then forbade binocular use. This developed into a sharp shower from which the young cock sought shelter while his sister chose a high and exposed perch as though enjoying the sensation of rain spots falling on her plumage. Eventually, both got quite wet, requiring a comprehensive preen to restore order when the sun came out again. During the clearance both flew continuously, to the evident discomfiture of a jay trying to preen bedraggled feathers in the top of the riven tree. Now that the adult merlins were away for so much of the time, it became clear that this tree was used habitually by a number of birds and was the centre of the solitary magpie's territory. For the juveniles, the magpie gave not a fig. While the jay ducked, dodged and shifted perches nervously, the pie went about its business wholly unconcerned.

The day developed into one of showers separated by bright intervals. For the birds, a succession of wettings and plumage maintenance. At 4.30, the curlews pottered about on their bog, accompanied by one offspring identifiable as such by its much shorter bill. At 5.00, during the best clearance of the afternoon, the freshly preened merlins went aloft for more of their attack and evasion routines. While they were up there, a large wisp of sheepswool blew across a stretch of bare gound. The young male fell at it like an arrowhead and hit it first time. Rising vertically with it, he opened his talons and let it fall, tipping over to stoop at a passing crow with equal vigour and greater venom.

The crow avoided a raked back by making a violent twisting shift; the young hen merlin beat purposefully towards its mate, following in line astern. Both crows flew on up-valley, each with its attendant merlin. 150yd to the left of the big oak the merlins broke off their pursuit, the crows landed to investigate the vegetation in peace. The merlins thus proclaimed what they at this stage regarded as their defended territory. In shape, it was an ellipse, with the nest tree – the one tree in which they no longer perched – standing well towards the left of it; *not* in the centre.

Two more spells of fighter tactics followed, the second ending in a race for the rocks where the adult male was thus revealed standing over a kill. His daughter won the ensuing tug-of-war and carried the prey to the ground beneath a tree directly in front of us. The wind blew freshly along the hillside as she bowed to tear and feed. There was no stream of feathers drifting down-wind, from which we conjectured that the kill may have been, untypically, furred prey – from its size, a mouse or vole.

At 5.50, half an hour later, the cock visited the site again. This time his son was the beneficiary. Although the young female could not have been troubled by hunger, she challenged her brother for possession and took an unusually long time to settle down afterwards. Perhaps furred prey, according to her notions, did not really count as food!

Eventually, she flew to the ground to hunt for insects. The magpie which had watched these events closely from its perch in the riven tree, took off and approached the merlin low and stealthily from the rear. It alighted briefly on a tussock just up the gradient from her, then landed squarely on her back to drive a rain of blows at her nape, then grasp at the cervical area of her spine. The merlin, screaming and flailing her wings, broke away from under the magpie and fled, making for a group of thorns which stood close together 30yd away. Into these she retreated and disappeared from view. The fact that she flew strongly and under normal control suggested that any injuries suffered were superficial. Or so we hoped.

Ten minutes later, she flew to the top of the riven tree. Down among its roots, the magpie pottered and probed. When one focused binoculars on the riven tree, a small dead tree beside it was also in view. In the top of this sat the other youngster. He muted lavishly (for the fourth time that day, giving evidence thereby of the abundance of his diet) raised his wings above his back, lowered them, roused, fell without further warning in an arrowhead stoop upon the grounded magpie. He struck it hard, knocking it over on its side, then continued on his way. The pie lay fluttering feebly for a minute or more; the merlin alighted on the top of a thorn-bush, then wormed his way inside the foliage.

Except for birds entering or occupying a nest tree, I had never before seen any merlin go *inside* a tree or bush. Always, they had perched on an outside branch. Again, one is driven by events to reconsider the part played in the affairs of birds by intelligence as opposed to simple instinct. The bird had behaved in a manner appropriate to conceptual thinking; the use of imagination to visualise a counter-attack by the magpie and the intelligent use of a stratagem to frustrate it. If the merlin were among the habitually harried and hunted, this behaviour might be accounted for reasonably in terms of instinct alone. But they are not. *They* are the hunters; fearlessness the keynote of their characters. Sheer coincidence might explain the sequence of events; equally, it might not.

At 6.30, the cock brought in another kill, calling his offspring to somewhere out of sight in the valley bottom for the surrender of it. Shortly afterwards we left rather uneasily, aware that the hobby had not shown up once, although the wind had blown all day from a quarter which had previously led it to hunt the ridge above the merlin site in full view of our OP. Sightings on the 18th had calmed our fears, but on the assumption that soaked and chilled nestlings would succumb rapidly. It seemed highly probable, but it was still only an assumption. Being unaware of even the approximate location of its nest – if any – all we could do was make conjectures and hope that time would bring clarification.

The next morning differed but little from its predecessor. A gusty wind still blew from the west, with a threat of further showers. Both young merlins were noisy and active, dispelling any residual doubts about damage which the magpie might have inflicted on the hen. At 11.40 there was a light shower, but swifts continued to wheel high over the valley, confirming their faith in the essential benevolence of the day's weather. At 11.45 the cock arrived, called, and presented a kill to his son who flew to him to receive it. At 12.15 clamour broke out. The cock flew in again, moving from tree to tree, his daughter in pursuit, squealing her appeals for lunch. For once, he had come empty handed. Dropping from his last perch, he flew fast and straight towards the spur, the young hen following. He flew on; she dropped on to the top of a low thorn right on the skyline. There she sat calling for several minutes, but would follow her sire no farther.

Instead, she flew back to the riven tree. Watching her fly, I picked up her brother on a converging course. They flew into the topmost branches ... where their father was already perched, still empty handed. We were getting the full treatment: 'Now you sees me: now you don't.' But clearly, something new was afoot. An attempt to lead the young away from the nest and out over the moor, for hunting tuition, perhaps? But as yet they were unready to go. After anxious clamour indicative of confusion and conflicting impulses, both eventually settled down in the riven tree, perched side by side.

At 1.10, the third and final attempt at my decapitation was made. Again, the low flying raptor was on exactly the same course. The hobby? No. A cock merlin. A cock merlin which, in a manner of speaking, passed right under my nose. It was rangy with exceptionally long wings and a long tail which was plain as a roof-slate except for the subterminal bar. It continued down the hill unperturbed by the encounter, crossed the valley, and zig-zagged up the opposite slope checking every patch of cover as it went. It was hunting, for sure. The youngsters sat tight without a murmur. The penny dropped. This was the cock merlin of the second sighting made on the very first day the valley was visited. A second cock merlin indeed, in every sense of the word. A second cock . . . a second pair, a second family? There might well be two pairs of merlins breeding on these hills; and not so very far apart at that. The place was growing into a veritable gold-mine of rare raptors. What next, I wondered?

But that proved to be the high spot of the day. The young birds remained in view; there was a food presentation at 2.25, when, while following the young male in flight, I was led by him to where his father was in the act of surrendering a cock whinchat to his daughter. At 4.00 I left. Again, there was no hint of the hobby. Between 2.30 and my departure there had been a long period of total inactivity. Very odd. A blustering wind from the west on Saturday had inspired bout after bout of fighter tactics: the same conditions prevailing on Sunday had been ignored absolutely. Such is birdwatching.

16

Education

25 July was still and humid. There was no greeting when we arrived in the OP, but Tatty, the kestrel of unusually ragged plumage, was up over the crest demonstrating that the atmosphere, thick and displeasing to the human skin though it was, conveyed more lift than seemed likely.

Had the young merlins gone by this time? In fifteen minutes the question was answered. The young hen came circling up from low on the opposite hillside and soared high, calling. Then she attempted to mob Tatty, who evaded her stoops with ease, despite disordered aerofoils. Eventually, she dropped into the heather on the ridge behind us. It was the first time we had seen either young merlin on our side of the valley. Would the OP continue to be an OP, we wondered? Should we move? But where? If the vicinity of the big oak and the trees nearby had lost their magnetic attraction the show was virtually over. Chasing merlins on foot through such terrain would be like trying to pick needles from a haystack blindfolded and wearing boxing gloves.

But soon, both birds were calling in flight over the horizon behind, working along it towards the head of the valley. Rounding this, they followed the line of the opposite crest to end up on familiar perches. On these and other tree perches in the vicinity they remained quietly for the best part of two hours.

Then the cock arrived, carrying prey. But this time he did not follow his usual practice of landing and calling the juveniles to him. Instead, he circled in the valley at high speed, carrying the prey, calling sharply, evading the clumsy stoops made at him by both youngsters. Having striven to inculcate the principle that a full crop is the reward of pursuit and attack, he eventually surrendered the kill to one of them. Which one was not clear.

During the next two and a half hours the weather improved.

The air dried out, a pleasant breeze sprang up, clouds rode higher in the sky. But there was little sign of birds responding, the only event being the arrival of the mistlethrush flock, now twenty strong.

At 4.35 the cock merlin arrived; flying fast along the valley, about half-way up the opposite slope. His daughter flew a parallel course, a little higher, calling for the kill he carried. Evading her, he presented it quickly to her brother. There was no attempt this time to lure either youngster into a pursuit; no tantalisation. The young hen, her disappointment audible, flew to a tall tree near the skyline where a redstart squared up to her defiantly. After making a forlorn and incredibly clumsy attempt at catching it, she flew to the far rocks where she flopped about in the bracken, often with wings half spread, hunting insects. His meal concluded, her brother flew over to tempt her into the sky for battle practice. She joined him readily, but one or the other broke away in less than a minute to make a determined attack on a passing woodpigeon which the pigeon paid it the compliment of taking seriously. The pigeon having been put to flight, its attacker made repeated stoops at the other young merlin, now perched in the top of one of a circle of small thorns over towards the spur. After each stoop it levelled off to rise vertically, on an even keel, as though attached by an invisible wire to a high-speed winch directly overhead.

The breeze was light, the thermals unremarkable. Kestrels, up over the ridges most of the day, had to fan their wings to hover. Yet the merlin, merely by use of the effects of this gently moving air, could rise effortlessly on absolutely motionless pinions. Kites, buzzards and kestrels, whose way of life keeps them on the wing for hours on end, display their skills generously. Bird-hawks, who may do the day's business in a matter of minutes, do not. But the skills are there when required, in ample measure.

The buzzing had the desired effect. Number 2 circled up to play. This time the game was not so much one of agile attack and evasion as of perfect station-keeping in a series of sophisticated manoeuvres. Stooping; rising vertically; side-slipping; even when allowing the wind to carry them backwards, the birds kept perfect station, as though linked by a rigid but unseen tow-bar. At the time, I was puzzled by the object of this game. Enlightenment came later.

While they were up, the deportment of the mistlethrushes was subdued. After a brief rest, the merlins soared up again. A young mistlethrush broke from cover and flew along the hillside. In a flash, the young cock was after it. No game this time; there was no mistaking the deadly earnest of its intention. The thrush was quickly aware of its plight and put on steam: the merlin flung itself into a fantastic burst of acceleration, wings flickering in a blur. But prematurely: before it had closed to anywhere near grasping distance, the hawk was tiring; the rate of overtake visibly diminishing. Suddenly, the quarry, too, was spent and the gap between the two birds began to close again, fast. But succour was at hand, the exhausted thrush having reached the bushes where half the flock was perched. Up they went, in a cloud, scattering in all directions. The young merlin, confused by the sudden proliferation of targets, struck twisting and flashing in all directions; distracted from every attack by other targets moving within apparently easier reach.

Breaking off, he dropped into a thorn-bush to perch with head sunk between hunched shoulders in what we had come to recognise as the merlin's gesture of defeat, humiliation and emotional withdrawal. It was a temporary withdrawal, however. A redstart emerged from low down in the bush and attempted to depart the scene unnoticed. Like an arrow from a bow, the merlin was after it. The redstart dived for the valley bottom and the cover of the thick vegetation bordering the stream; it whirled away at the last moment and climbed again for the thorn-bushes it had so imprudently left. The merlin stuck to it like glue; twisting, snatching, missing. Down went the redstart again, headlong. Down went the merlin, stooping with furled wings to close the gap reopened by the smaller bird's unforeseen manoeuvre. Both birds passed out of sight below the hillside where it bulged out beneath the OP. As far as we could judge, the merlin did not reappear within the next half-hour. We could not be certain, because a merlin in flight which does not attract attention by calling can easily be missed; but the chances were more than even that we had witnessed a pursuit which had at last resulted in a kill.

One thing was beyond dispute and tended to confirm last year's conjectures. Attempts were certainly made by young merlins to exploit a richly stocked larder left for them by their parents in the vicinity of the nest.

But which of the youngsters had made these sterling efforts? As far as we could judge, it was the cock, using, perhaps, the advantage conferred by twenty-four extra hours of develop-ment. The feebleness of the attempt on the redstart made by his sister earlier reinforced this conclusion.

28 July was warm and humid, and what little breeze there was blew from the north-east. Our arrival was delayed until midday and celebrated by an immediate soaring flight by both juveniles. We had not watched them at such close quarters as the 1972 birds, or since so early in their history. But our attendances had been more frequent and there was growing reason to suspect that curiosity and interest were becoming reciprocal, if only faintly so from the birds' side of the valley.

On this occasion, however, we were treated to a lengthy scrutiny from high overhead, which developed into a display of fighter tactics culminating in a long steep peregrine-like stoop aimed by brother at sister. This she evaded by falling to the trees below, where her brother immediately joined her.

Two large flights of homing pigeons twinkled in the sky over the ridge. A tiny dark shape fell at them from high above, like a stone. In mounting excitement, I raised the binoculars. It wanted only this to set the final seal on the dream-like character of the valley. The bird, obviously too small to be a falcon peregrine, must be a tiercel. As it grew in size in the binocular window it also became ruddier in hue. A *young* tiercel? A bird of the year? Passing clean through the pigeon flock, it came headlong at us to bang down in the heather but 30yd to the right of our OP. It was an extremely handsome young kestrel, every feather in perfect order. We had made the acquaintance of a bird we were shortly to dub 'Super-Kes' and had been reminded again that surprise may await the serious bird-watcher round any corner.

Across the valley, the merlins were now perched high in the riven tree, attended by a family party of wood warblers which took remarkable liberties with equally remarkable impunity. Unaware, it seemed, of the lethal potentialities of their larger neighbours when immobile, the little birds searched the twigs and leaves for insects and spiders almost to where the talons of the young merlins gripped the bark. One, fluttering from spray to spray, hovered for a moment as though the head of the young merlin nearest to it was to be used as a perch. When, instead, it alighted beside her, response was confined to a basilisk stare.

At 2.00 a merlin came along the ridge, flying fast and calling in unmistakeable accents. Mamma again; at last, the positively brown tint of her wings and back contrasting with the nondescript hue of her offspring. She dropped into a tree on the crest and preened her breast-feathers, at first to be ignored. Then, with an outburst of clamour, both flew to her, demanding food or attention. Taking not the slightest notice of them, she rose from the tree to soar high directly over the valley. Having reached her pitch, she gave a display of aerobatics which underlined with emphasis the difference between adult and juvenile merlin skills, however advanced the latter may be.

For a split second, she was joined by her mate. Approaching her in a shallow dive, he slipped beneath her, rolled on his back, extended his legs. Briefly, they touched talons; and he was gone. She soared higher still, eventually to sail away down-valley a mere speck in the sky.

Half an hour later, events took place in a puzzling sequence. The young cock left his perch to fly fast and purposefully to a small tree right at the head of the valley, just round on the shoulder which developed into the slope where we sat. Immediately, another merlin, appearing out of the blue, dropped into the heather beside the tree. Simultaneously, juvenile merlin calls rang out from across the valley directly in front. The bird which had joined the young male at the head of the valley had not looked like an adult, but such we presumed it must have been. Next, although no birds had been seen in flight, both the young merlins were found together again, perched in a low bush.

A sheep came galloping downhill towards the bush, bleating frantically. Why it did so was not apparent, but Welsh border hill sheep often display such symptoms of dementia. Evidently under a delusion that such phenomena as falcon-eating sheep roamed the uplands, both young merlins took off in panic; but the cock recovered his dignity by turning sharply to buzz the animal angrily before joining his sister in seeking a less troubled perch. Having dissipated their surplus adrenalin in a brief spell of fighter tactics, both birds alighted farther down the slope in a bushy thorn tree already occupied by the magpie. Its consternation was plain to see as it poked its head in and out of the lower foliage trying to make up its mind on the safest course to adopt. Eventually, it emerged from the far side of the tree – the direction in which the merlins were not at the time looking – to march smartly away via several bracken patches which offered a measure of concealment. Times had indeed changed since the day of the murderous assault.

Shortly afterwards, the young cock took off to fly up-valley, climbing like a rocket, and was locked a moment later in combat with another hawk. Such was the speed of stoop, evasion and counter-stoop that there was for a moment or two difficulty in deciding the identity of the other bird, which proved eventually to be a young kestrel of remarkable gifts and self-possession.

But what was going on? The merlin was far from achieving the usual push-over victory. Rather the reverse: its extra half inch or so of tail used to proper effect appeared to give the kestrel a slight edge of manoeuvrability. The tables were turned. The issue had ceased to be one of merlin mobbing kestrel, or even attempting to do so. The kestrel had gained the upper hand over a tiring and plainly confused young merlin. Only with the greatest of difficulty could it dodge well-aimed wing buffets, delivered with confident determination.

Squeaking like a downy nestling, the merlin fled the battlefield to take refuge low in a thorn-bush. There he sat; his head sunk deep between his shoulders like a little owl.

The kestrel swept up to soar and circle over the valley in triumph. Coffee cups were raised in salute. Super-Kes received his – or her – baptism.

Bent on the restoration of family honour, the young hen merlin climbed to the attack. Super-Kes saw her coming and soared away from her as though the merlin had been handicapped by the attachment of lead weights to her feet. Labouring on, the young merlin persisted in her efforts, but in vain. The harder she tried to gain altitude, the faster the kestrel rose above her. Eventually, she abandoned the attempt and returned to the hillside where she and her brother flew from tree to tree squeaking as though aware of their humiliation.

One did not need to be clairvoyant to appreciate that the recovery of their *amour propre* would shortly require some unsuspecting creature to get an undeserved come-uppance. It – or they – proved to be a pair of carrion crows which got away unscathed, but by only a narrow margin. Feeling visibly better, the merlins climbed skywards to celebrate their rehabilitation with more fighter tactics. That accomplished, they shared the upper sprays of a small tree in the thorn circle towards the spur.

Having watched them preen thoroughly, I lowered the binoculars; to pick up immediately, with the naked eye, a merlin in flight which seemed to be neither the adult hen nor cock as it made its way towards them low over the ground. As it flew, it took bites at an insect held in one foot. Seeing it, the youngsters broke into frantic clamour, fluttering around in their tree-top. The bird in flight was certainly not the adult cock; but there was an odd cast of grey in its upper plumage singularly inappropriate to the hen. To confuse the issue still further, the bird fell to the ground at the foot of the tree, wings spread, squeaking an appeal to be fed by 'our' young merlins! It was identical to them in all respects except for a rather rangier outline. All three took off, and circled the tree in evident excitement. Twice more, the newcomer fell to the ground on spread wings and went through the food-begging routine. Ultimately, the residents lost interest and the newcomer flew up-valley to perform a competent display flight over an area to which they laid no claim.

So it was not just a matter of a second adult male on the hills. It was another breeding pair – and progeny. The odd comings and goings earlier in the day suddenly fell into place. This had not been the *first* appearance of the third juvenile!

After its flight, it settled in a flat-topped tree well up-valley from the territory of the residents. Its departure was missed due to alternative entertainment offered by the young male at the time. Suddenly, in flight, he began to shadow-box; or so it seemed until I saw the cabbage butterfly he was trying to catch. The erratic dancing flight of a butterfly makes it an extremely difficult target for a bird belonging to a family which achieves most of its kills by a correct assessment of exactly where a prey will be a tenth of a second hence. Twisting and turning, hovering and backing, the merlin snatched and clutched in vain as the butterfly rose and fell, veered and fluttered unpredictably. Finally, he hauled off 30yd to circle up and come back in a shallow powered stoop with force sufficient to stun a 20lb turkey. He caught his butterfly . . . but opening his talons to alight in the riven tree, lost it again. Without a moment's hesitation, the butterfly resumed its interrupted mating dance; the object of its affections having followed her captured swain as he made his involuntary journey to the riven tree. And she followed so swiftly that she was there on the spot at the very instant the merlin lost his hard-won prey.

The hawk shrunk into itself: head buried between despairing shoulders. There are some days when just *nothing* goes right. While recovery from this new disappointment took its natural and unhurried course, his sister occupied herself in searching for insects among the bilberries on the spur. Presently, she flew into a thorn and called her brother, who joined her immediately.

The young curlew, whose lengthening bill would soon deny us the evidence by which to recognise him for what he was, was also engaged upon a search for food among the bilberries. He became the next target, having to duck stoop after stoop and bending his legs as he did so until he was virtually crouched on the ground. It seemed that he strove to appear unintimidated, but compulsive preening resorted to between the assaults suggested otherwise. Sensibly, though, the curlew resisted any impulse felt to take refuge in immediate flight, walking instead downhill, unhurried and halting for refreshment here and there until the attacks were abandoned. Then and only then, he flew away to leave the valley entirely.

The trouble with juvenile merlins, we began to feel, was a total inability to recognise targets appropriate to their powers.

The merlins fidgeted from perch to perch, with spells of insect hunting in the bilberries and bracken. While the cock was perched on the top of a small thorn, a meadow pipit flew by. Having wasted two invaluable seconds in rousing and leg-flexing, he took off in pursuit. The pipit reached the cover of a bracken patch and dived in, the merlin thumping down after it like a kestrel dropping on a vole. Thrashing up out of the deep bracken, it hovered for a second or two, then crashed in again. And a third time. As it rose for a fourth attempt, another pipit flew by, dipping and rising in undulations as so many small birds do when making flights of more than a few yards. Strenuously, the merlin beat up after it, but the pipit was going with the wind and escaped with ease.

Both young merlins resumed their insect hunting; the female so far forgetting her station in life as to scratch like a domestic hen. The day declined towards evening without further drama, the only fresh event an attack on the magpie, which lost no time in seeking cover. A pigeon, bilberrying downhill from the bush on which the merlins were at the time perched, invited attack; but none was made. Perhaps experience was beginning to teach the young falcons something of their limitations. It was to be hoped that instinct and practice would soon teach them to catch birds of the size their species traditionally preyed on. In six hours there had been not a single parental contribution to their upkeep.

17
Finale

There could be no question that our merlin-watching days in 1973 were now numbered.

There were also more serious considerations. Did the six-hour parental absence on the 28th mean that the youngsters were now cast off to stand on their own two feet or perish? A critical stage in the saga had been reached; observations on as continuous a basis as possible should be valuable.

So on the 29th we were back, a little earlier in the day than usual. At 10.30 the sun shone fiercely from a clear blue sky; a faint breath of wind came sporadically from the north-east. As I approached the OP, alone on this occasion, young merlins called. The young cock passed directly overhead, coming from the moor up behind the OP. Five minutes later, the hen flew in on a parallel course but farther down the valley. A pipit flew past her brother within talon-grasp but did not provoke any reaction. Presumably the merlin had fed.

Super-Kes floated in to perch on a rock near the bush where the young hen sat. Neither did that provoke a reaction. Then a raven arrived to perch in a nearby tree, also without interference: a sure indication that the adult merlins were not at hand. But ten minutes later, there was clamour. Merlins seemed to be flashing everywhere. When the confusion resolved itself the adult male was flying away up-valley and one juvenile was in hot pursuit of the other around trees, bushes and rocks. It transpired that the hen was the bird pursued, her brother the pursuer. Eventually shaking him off, she settled to feed. He found a new stump to perch on, from which he protested noisily for ten minutes. So his neglect of the opportunity to try for the pipit was not, after all, the consequence of a full crop. More evidence of this was provided by a second attempt to steal or share his sister's loot.

Whatever took place did so out of sight behind a tree, but not inaudibly. After a few minutes, the young cock flew to a high perch. His sister tried to join him, flying heavily. Such an ill-judged job was her touch-down that she narrowly avoided landing plumb on top of him. Falling from the tree, she recovered near the ground to flap owlishly to a lower perch. There she sat with bulging crop, risking regurgitation as she bent double to clean her toes meticulously.

Movement attracted my attention. It was the cock, engaged in something more exciting than the delivery of food. He was actually hunting a pipit right there on the hillside. I shall never know whether the bird, in its attempts to escape from him, had led the cock to his own valley, or whether he hunted there with ulterior motive. But what a masterly performance! If the intention was, as I suspect, to give a lesson in fieldcraft to the two youngsters now providing an excited audience, they could not, it seemed, have had a more expert tutor.

Deadly economy of effort was the keynote of his technique. No dashing wildly hither and thither; just a relentless paced pursuit, such as good hunting dog or weasel might have used to wear down the quarry. Speed was employed for one purpose only; to flash into the out-field to cut the pipit off from any promising patch of cover they drew near. Then, the acceleration was phenomenal. The merlin was clearly so much a master of its craft that the outcome must be a mere matter of time – measured in seconds. Any moment now, the pipit would tire, visibly: the merlin would move in for a kill which would be made to look as effortless as a pigeon plucking a bilberry. A mathematical inevitability. But somehow, despite the wizardry of the master, the pipit had worked its way to where two cover options were open to it. One uphill; one downhill: one a cluster of rowans, the other a dense patch of bracken. Even a merlin cannot contrive to be in two places at once. The pipit feinted at the rowans, the merlin deflected in a flash to cut off that line of retreat. In the tenth part of a second which it took the merlin to get there, the pipit turned and dived into the bracken. The merlin reversed its course faster than the eye could follow, flung up, stooped in after it. Emerging empty-handed, it crashed down again and again. Son and daughter veered and circled overhead, hysterical with excitement.

While the cock continued to hammer the bracken patch, the pipit crept out of it on foot, ran downhill unnoticed and flew into a dense thorn-bush. Accepting his failure philosophically, the cock flew away fast down the valley, calling over his shoulder to the youngsters to follow him. This time, they did; and suddenly, appearing as though by magic, the hen, too, was flying across the hillside, following on behind.

Super-Kes appeared on the scene. It transpired that he (or she) was Tatty's offspring, because Tatty promptly caught a vole somewhere up at the back of the OP and surrendered it. There was more virtuoso flying by this remarkable young kestrel, concluded by a 100ft falling side-slip across the wind which took it straight to a feather-light touch-down on what amounted to no more than a twig protruding from the ground.

At 12.15 the young cock merlin returned, coming in low and fast. He perched in a tree high up the hillside, to be mobbed amicably by a flock of swallows. Although untroubled by their attentions, he seemed to take a keen interest in the smaller birds unrelated to their possible status as prey. Perhaps the similarity of silhouette in flight to his own, apart from their forked tails, accounted for this. All along, there had been suggestions that shape meant more to young merlins than size or colour. Between 1.00 and 1.30 he flew restlessly from tree to tree, showing the usual signs of disquiet displayed when his sister was absent. Eventually he flew to a tree in which she sat perched, having entered the valley undetected.

Tatty alighted on a nearby tree: both the young merlins flew to her immediately, begging frantically to be fed. A fortnight out of the nest and still no clear conception of their precise relationship to their parents and other hawks.

Today, many mating pairs of white butterflies fluttered over the valley. Capriciously, the merlins chose to ignore them. At 2.20, the young cock moved to a different tree, but tensed on alighting, crouched, and fell in an arrowhead stoop at a woodpigeon perched in the top of a tree lower down the slope. He missed it narrowly, but did not pursue. Taking off again suddenly, he flew fast up-valley, his new target an incoming carrion crow. But after one vicious buzz he broke off to make a renewed attack on the woodpigeon, now on the ground trying to feed. Missing it, he chattered angrily and flew back to his original tree. Half an hour later, he and his sister together made a third attack on the hapless bird as it tried to leave the valley peacefully, its crop bulging with bilberries.

Their next flight took them to the spur, where the young hen hunted insects on the ground. A chaffinch landed in a bush 5yd away and conveniently down the slope from the perch occupied by the young cock. It had not seen him. Perversely, he stared at it; roused, tensed, relaxed. The bird was allowed to fly away unpursued and unscathed.

Unexpectedly, he launched himself skywards, climbed fast, then levelled off, trying to hover. After a moment's bewilderment, I spotted his quarry, a large, high-flying crane fly. This he eventually caught as he caught the butterfly – by drawing off some distance and stooping at it. He soared with it held negligently in one foot as his sister circled up towards him in stealthy silence. Zooming up beneath him, she rolled over on her back, shot out a foot and failed to steal his catch by only the narrowest of margins. Startled by the attack, the young cock climbed away fast to eat the insect out of his foot as he flew.

At 4.30, yikking stridently, both young merlins left their perch on the spur to fly straight at me with what looked at first like deadly intent. Fame at last: I was to be the subject of an appendix note in the next edition of *The Merlin's Handbook*: 'A notable recent addition to the already extensive list of prey items known to have been taken by merlins is a large male ornithologist.'

But the object of their enthusiasm was Tatty, feeding another vole to Super-Kes on the hillside behind me. For this they competed as vociferously as usual, but, without avail.

At this point I lost them, to rediscover one of them ten minutes later in hot and clamorous pursuit of a bird I at first took for its father. But no; it was the hobby – at last. As it passed, a little below eye-level, it shifted up a gear and left the young merlin standing, as it were, to pester the empty air where it had been flying a bare moment before. Never had I seen a bird move so fast in level flight. Losing its pursuer, it found a thermal at the head of the valley. In this, it spiralled up and up – and up. For five minutes it rose, without a single movement of its outstretched wings, until 12×60 binoculars recorded it as but a tiny speck in the sky. From this immense height it started to fall, slowly at first, then more steeply. Finally, it dropped below the western horizon in a vertical stoop at incalculable speed. That western horizon was now darkening with thunderheads black enough to command a prompt withdrawal. Again, I rushed back to the car and escaped the storm by seconds.

On 1 August, another day of boiling heat, I did not see the young merlins at all; but the day was not devoid of interest. At 10.15, a merlin alighted in a tree on the opposite ridge, but such was the blue film of heat haze that the only certainty was the fact that the bird was not an adult male. A pair of chaffinches joined it in the tree; then a wood warbler and a cock redstart. They held a protest meeting during which the warbler, recalling the incident of 28 July, seemed at one stage about to perch on the falcon's head. Whether this kamikaze spirit is common to wood warblers I cannot say. Perhaps it accounts in part for their limited distribution. Eventually, the merlin left, flying towards the next tree along the ridge. On the way there, she deflected with the speed of greased lightning to catch an insect I failed to see. This she ate quickly on reaching her destination. With the light falling on her from a fresh angle, I saw that it was the adult hen. When she left, she flew low up-valley and fast, with powerful rowing wing strokes.

Half an hour later, she was back, preening in the tree on the ridge. This completed, she took off to fly directly towards me. Noticing me somewhat belatedly, she turned sharply away and flew to a thorn on the spur. There, she was immediately buzzed by another, and paler, hen merlin which flew on in deadly swift pursuit of a young mistlethrush which had made the possibly fatal error of flying up out of the bilberries at that very moment.

So, in the end, I had made the acquaintance of all members of both families, as with dispersal territorial considerations had faded into the background. 'My' hen kept me company for much of the day, preening incessantly. Frequently she spread her tail in a wide fan, as if to say: 'Look. It *is* me. No white tips.'

Late in the afternoon, the hobby came again, but again not hunting. Finding a thermal with ease, it soared beautifully and rose to an immense height. Sitting there between these magnificent birds I had some inkling of the dilemma of a judge at a dressage competition. I, however, was under no compulsion to announce a verdict.

Again, the flight of the hobby, which had on this occasion begun right before me at less than eye-level, ended with an accelerating stoop from a height at which it had become a mere speck in the sky. But what did this pattern of behaviour signify? Had the young been lost in the deluge? Or had they now fledged and been left to the care of their father, as had the young merlins, once they were out and about? From the slight rounding of the extremities of the wing tips, the bird was plainly a female hobby.

Methodical birdwatching answers many questions – but gives rise to as many to which the answers are never found.

As it turned out, this was to be my last sighting of both the hobby and the hen merlin.

On the 5th, a day of poor light diffused in a sky of weird cloud formation, the young merlins were back in the valley, calling but unseen until mid-afternoon. Then, at 3.00, one flew the length of the hillside in good view. Although I did not know it, that was the farewell. Plover gathering into flocks underlined the fact that summer was drawing to its close. The last visit of all was made on 11 August, a day or two before the guns arrived.

At 3.50, the cock merlin sped along the skyline: at 6.30 we decamped; leaving the valley to Tatty, Super-Kes, newly arrived buzzards and many coveys of grouse feeding in happy ignorance of what the immediate future held in store for them.

THE FOURTH YEAR

18

Beginnings

Knowing that little is usually to be gained there beyond eyes streaming with wind-tears and fingers too numb to rotate the focusing-wheel of the binoculars, I do not include the high moors in my winter-time birdwatching programme. But in December 1973 I made an exception to the rule, prompted by a whim to sample the mid-winter atmosphere of the merlin site watched that summer.

The upper valley lay silent and deserted; but on the shoulders the dormant heather retained sufficient of its summer population of meadow pipits to arouse surprise. Both pipits and the occasional neat pile of freshly plucked pipit feathers were there, responsibility for which seemed likely to rest with roving sparrowhawks from the oak woods below.

We explored the valley from the head to where at the mouth a clump of old larches stands erect, as though on sentry-duty, on the steep valley wall. Sharper eyes than mine were first to see a dull brown bird quartering the rough pasture below. 'Look there – over that light-coloured pocket-handkerchief bit of meadow: a buzzard, isn't it?' The finger pointed clearly, the description was apt. As the glasses focused, a blast of Arctic wind blinded me for the moment. Blinking to clear the sudden tears, I saw the bird distinctly for a split second before it passed into dead ground. Long, broad, spread-fingered wings; a long tail, boldly barred, and a white rump. My son had seen his first hen harrier.

We settled down for the next hour on an observation post commanding the pocket-handkerchief meadow, some of the lower valley, the lands below, but not the clump of larches. The hillside bulged out beneath us, hiding ground one would have preferred to have under observation. Unfortunate, but unavoidable in the circumstances. In terrain of that nature, there is always some desirable patch of ground obscured by the lie of the land. As the light gave its first hint of fading, a small hawk dashed into view and out again beneath the overhang, moving too fast for glasses to be raised, let alone focused. Brown above; with the odd feather edged buff. Rusty-gold below, the angle such that neither wing nor tail length could be determined with confidence.

Presumably an immature cock spar; but a spark of speculation had been ignited. With so many pipits overwintering on the moor, had the merlins any cause to fly south? Was the bird in fact an immature merlin? Colours, as they had been glimpsed, might apply to either species. The use of plodding human feet to overtake one equipped with the swift wings of a raptor proved as futile as ever, but there are matters in which experience never teaches. One always hopes that the bird has perched only just out of sight: such hopes invariably deceive, as they did on that occasion.

'I wouldn't mind scrambling down to the valley bottom and climbing the opposite shoulder,' announced a voice powered by lungs with over twenty years less wear and tear to their debit. As I concealed my private misgivings, we descended the precipitous slope. And it was not I who tobogganed 5yd on his rump after his foot slipped on a patch of mud.

The stream ran full but clear. The sky was cloudless: the light fading but luminous. In the valley bottom, the air was still. From the larches, a big bird flapped lazily up, set its wings in a shallow sharp-angled W and soared. It was the hen harrier, every feather-marking picked out in detail by the rays of the setting sun. Delicately adjusting the spread and flex of its sensitive tail, the graceful hawk from the north cut tight circles directly above, turning its head inwards to keep us under careful observation. Eventually, it side-slipped across the wind, gliding away over the shoulder we were shortly to climb, to be seen no more that day or afterwards.

Naturally, these events inspired more winter visits. One took place on a day of grey cloud scudding before a bitter wind which threatened snow; a wind used by a hen sparrowhawk to outclimb with ease a family party of ravens ascending to mob her. Eventually, the glasses located a small falcon high over a ridge a thousand yards distant. It fell like a stone to vanish instantly against the background of the winter-brown hillside. It was merlin behaviour; but one could overlook neither the probable presence nor the known virtuosity of the young Super-Kes.

Three visits failed to rediscover the harrier and to establish with certainty that merlins had remained on the hills through the winter – or, perhaps, that the territories of the breeding population had been taken over for the winter by other merlins which had flown south from harsher lands in the distant north.

The site was not visited again until March. Pipits were busy in the establishment of their territories; unarguable kestrels hovered over the ridges. Grouse called, ordering instant departure. A pair of sportive ravens linked feet high overhead, failed to disengage in time, crash-landed in the heather with no apparent ill effect. On the merlin site, no bird but the curlews was yet in residence and these protested vigorously at the intrusion.

The 1973 site was visited again on 21 April. Blackbird, wren, chaffinch and willow warbler were all in full song; the weather pleasantly spring-like as our most euphoric conventions could require. Two young men equipped with binoculars and telescopes sat high up the opposite shoulder, immediately above the nest-tree. Whether in awareness of the possibilities or by chance, I never discovered, but after an hour, at 12.25, they withdrew. At 12.35 merlins gave tongue, both screaming and 'yik-yikking', but the birds were not seen. At 1.55 there was more clamour: merlin calls and a hawk-noise of different timbre, during which Super-Kes soared up from the trees in the valley bottom to drift away over the moor, circle, and return to display unopposed over the valley.

At 2.15 the cock merlin flew in, banked away sharply to return whence he came. Whether the kestrel – again displaying – or the seated humans were responsible for this retreat, I am unable to say, but I suspect the latter. The suspicion grows in me that the time when it is most vital to avoid disturbing merlins is when they are in the course of selecting a breeding-site. Super-Kes, having for some minutes amused himself with attempts to catch an early-flying butterfly, fell to a tree 30yd down-valley from the merlins' site where another kestrel sat on a branch beside a second abandoned crows' nest.

The behaviour of the birds was that of a mating pair, but differences in their plumage were negligible, the sex of Super-Kes distinguishable by no more than a hint of grey on the rump. Otherwise, he was the virtual duplicate of his handsome young consort. An hour later, they attempted copulation on a pinnacle of rock; unsuccessfully, at first, the cock athwart the hen. After some minutes of fluttering frustration, instinct asserted itself and the task was accomplished. As the kestrels bound together at the climax of their coupling, a hen merlin called stridently. The plot, it seemed, was thickening.

Never before had I known a cock kestrel still in immature plumage to father a brood. If Super-Kes proved to be the exception, it would come as no great surprise, although certainly unforeseen. No less unexpected was the fact that he had been permitted to occupy territory held by merlins. His victory over a juvenile even younger than himself in 1973 was one thing: a challenge to an experienced adult male some years his senior another. Kestrels and merlins co-existently occupying old crows' nests in adjacent trees was a novel prospect. It seemed likely that Super-Kes, for all his 'alpha' qualities, was due shortly for a humiliating ejection.

There followed a long period of inactivity, but the excitements of the day were not over. A few minutes before 6.00, a raptor flashed past 10yd on my right, diving towards the valley bottom. Slate-grey were the wings and tail; but darker than those of the cock merlin seen earlier. Levelling out over the floor of the valley, the bird hurtled up the far shoulder, aiming for a thorn near the ridge, from which a blackbird had sung intermittently all day. With a squawk of terror, Blackie left the shelter of the bush, going out right as the handsome adult cock sparrowhawk – for such it was – banked round to the left of the bush, proclaiming his identity by showing us a plan-view of his distinctive silhouette before he climbed to close on his intended victim. Blackie, evidently no fool, sought safety in his marginally faster rate of climb, whirling away downwind and down-valley. The hawk accelerated his wing-beat, thrusting through the air in pursuit. The blackbird, also flying strongly, held a straight course; but his decision to put matters to the test in the open sky, far from cover, looked very like the indulgence of a death-wish.

Inexorably, as Blackie began to flag, the hawk closed the gap. Two silhouettes merged, the hawk rolling over, shooting out a foot and grabbing. Blackie, closing his wings, swooped, his target a patch of hawthorn scrub reaching up the shoulder 400yd away down-valley. A few dusky feathers danced in the air. Their former owner continued to fall like a stone, the hawk accelerating his following stoop with beaten wings.

An untimely veer in the breeze blew the hapless fugitive off-course at precisely the moment when escape began to seem a possibility. The pursuer, heavier and therefore more stable in a cross-wind, was suddenly between Blackie and the refuge he had sought so desperately. But the smaller bird lacked neither pluck nor the will to live. The hunter hung on the breeze for a critical split second, now uncertain of his prey's intention. Blackie used the fractional respite to turn back into the wind, again to try to outclimb his pursuer. Perhaps panic at finding his near-won retreat cut off after all had triggered a fresh shot of adrenalin. Suddenly, the blackbird no longer looked like a doomed loser. Both birds were now labouring visibly; the intended prey remaining stubbornly out of grasping distance, the hawk unable to reduce the gap between them, despite herculean efforts.

The birds now flew directly towards us, a little below eye-level. Travelling at an immense speed, they vanished beneath the overhang of the hillside. The voice of Blackie, who had maintained his frantic cackle of alarm throughout the chase, rose to a crescendo of agonised shrieks. I leaped down through the rocks and heather. Suddenly, the lower hillside was in view.

There, beneath a dense hawthorn, the sparrowhawk sprawled spread-eagled on the ground. From the bush came a subdued but still anxious peal of blackbird alarm-notes.

The hawk turned and lifted his head, glaring into the binoculars with mad yellow eyes. Gathering himself awkwardly, he beat up into the wind, legs hanging, talons empty. Blackie comforted his discomposure with a monologue of *sotto-voce* protest for the next half-hour, but when we left the scene at 7.00 he was back on his song perch, producing what was in the circumstances a praiseworthy declaration of proprietorship.

A kestrel of superior gifts: a pair of merlins: the possibility of one or more hobbies. Now a mature cock sparrowhawk hunting the valley. There seemed better places for a pair of blackbirds to set up home. One would not care to pay the premium on a personal-accident insurance policy for them.

19
Developments in Radnorshire

Two days later, the first visit of the season to the 1972 site was made. Encouraged by the remains of a newly killed ring ousel on the rim of the low cliffs, six hours were spent in patient vigil. They would have been marked by greater optimism had a few piles of pipit feathers also lined the cliff top.

The watch produced not a single incident of interest. No merlin: no living ring ousel. No wheatears: no whinchats. Even pipits were few and far between, much of the heather newly blighted. No buzzard soared; not a kestrel hung over the sky-line. A walk to rocks once harbouring the eyrie of peregrines, in whose shadow lay also a traditional merlin site in the heather, brought no greater success. There were jackdaws, stock doves, a solitary kestrel which hovered for half an hour without stooping once. The situation called for consultation.

My friend on the spot had interesting news to impart. Right over on the far side of the hills, a broad valley drains a virtually trackless moor. Hawthorns dot its slopes; rowans line the course of the stream and its small tributaries. There, on Easter Day, a cock merlin had been seen perched on the topmost spray of a tall thorn in which there was a crows' nest. The news confirmed a suspicion already held that this valley might at times be used. There, the last search conducted in 1973 had ended. On one shoulder there stretches a line of crumbling disused grouse-butts, several of which had been employed by some raptor as plucking posts. But the date was 3 June. Had merlins been in occupation, their presence should not have been in doubt. Perhaps I had overlooked them: more probably not. Local opinion, insofar as it was aware of the merlins, was unanimous in the conclusion that breeding had not been attempted in 1973. There had been no reports of display flights in spring, no juvenile sightings in summer or autumn.

With the uncertain position prevailing at the more northerly site, it was highly desirable to track down the Radnorshire birds. So 1 May found us wading thigh-deep in tall heather as we made our way to the lonely valley. Several steep dingles had to be traversed. Trees grew in all of them; crows had not neglected the opportunities presented. But all were vacant. Over one dingle, ravens circled proprietorially, but it was difficult to see where in such bland terrain they might have nested. Nevertheless, their unchallenged presence argued against the probability of merlins being in occupation. There was, however, plenty of moor still to be explored, including the valley of the principal watercourse.

Soon, the line of old grouse-butts came into view. Investigation of them, one by one, revealed a disappointing lack of recent kills. The last butt in the line formed a vantage point from which the whole valley could be scanned. The trees in valleys selected by nesting merlins usually form distinct, if open, thickets. Here, they were dotted about in isolation. In three of them, there were nests built in earlier years by crows. One was extremely near the top of an unusually tall hawthorn which occupied a commanding position on the hillside. From a patch of dense heather and bilberries among which modest comfort might be found, this tree could be watched from a suitable distance with those others which also contained crow's nests under remote observation. No merlin circled the area screaming as we drew nearer: hopes began to sink.

Last summer, it had seemed possible that in 1974 we might be embarrassed by knowing of more merlin sites than we had time to watch methodically. Now, it began to look as though the possibilities were slipping through our fingers. The Radnorshire birds removed to a still-undiscovered site; the situation in the northern valley bedevilled by the dominant presence of a kestrel lost to all sense of decorum. We settled down in the heather, two hundred yards up the slope from the tree, the nest a trifle below eye-level. A perfect position from which to watch; by far the best yet, should the nest be ear-marked for occupation. Obviously, it was not yet in use.

One hour and twenty minutes after our arrival, a merlin called sharply from somewhere out of sight up towards the head of the valley. A minute or two later, a hen flew in low, swept up to a perch in the tree-top, then worked her way down through the branches to settle on the nest. There she remained for the next three and a half hours, her presence betrayed by no more than the occasional flick of her tail and folded primaries. Both previous experience and what little was to be culled from reference works indicated that merlins did not lay much before the beginning of May. Experience had shown that incubation was shared by the pair in fairly short, if erratic, stints until the final week, when the hen sat for many hours unrelieved. What, then, were the possibilities? There were several, but by far the likeliest was that we had arrived on the very day that laying was in progress.

Half an hour before leaving, in thickening weather, an incident occurred which, although offering no immediate illumination, had significance later. A vivid blue cock merlin sped low across the moor. Not a sound was uttered; nor any attempt made to relieve the hen's long vigil. The bird was unquestionably hunting, using every fold in the ground to cover its approach, veering and jinking as a boxer bobs and weaves to conceal his real intention. All cover was buzzed to flush any possible occupant, no trick missed. A merlin hunting so near his nest site? Improbable, on previous showings.

On leaving the moor, we rated the chances of the birds being a true breeding pair no higher than 50/50. For all we knew to the contrary, a non-breeding hen merlin might take a fancy to brooding imaginary eggs. After all, there was the phenomenon of 'phantom pregnancy' among bitches and other mammals.

On 6 May all was made clear. More than that; it was one of those perfect days when the sun is bright but not dazzling, when high cloud and a fresh breeze signal the conditions in which the larger birds haunt the upper air as though it was their pleasure to be watched by their admirers. Birds and birdwatchers together thrill with invigoration.

My companion of the day is by birth an Englishman but a national of the United States by choice and adoption; yet one for whom the landscapes of our dwindling British wilderness have never lost their charm. Until that morning he had still to gaze upon his first merlin, despite a lifelong devotion to the observation of birds. Within five minutes of leaving the car, that anomaly had been remedied.

A cock merlin, kingfisher-blue in the morning light, planed down the hillside in pursuit of a songthrush. Flashing across the track in front of us, it skimmed a quickset hedge in which the quarry had found timely refuge, sped across the rising meadows on fast-flickering wings to melt into the horizon where rough grazing gave way to the heathery coast-line of the distant moor.

Our approach to the site was made circuitously to show to my friend all that the moor had to offer. Over a far ridge, four birds soared: buzzard and kestrel shadow-boxing without acrimony, a carrion crow mobbed a raven with a touch of it. Along the nearer crest, a hen sparrowhawk floated lethargically, ignoring the pipits which scurried from her approaching shadow. A pair of ring ousels displayed, leaving little doubt as to which cleft in the rowan-crowned rocks was destined to receive their patronage. Over a marshy pool high on the hill, black-headed gulls wheeled, rasped their shrill protest, and stooped boldly at the intruders. Redshank dashed among them, silent in their anxiety. A few breeding failures among the over-protected gulls would cause few tears to be shed, but the redshank merited consideration. As rapidly as possible, we increased the distance between ourselves and the disturbed waders.

Eventually, we topped a rise overlooking the head of the valley. A large pale brown hawk, oddly long in the tail, wafted mothlike along the opposite heather slope. Lazily, it made a pass at the ground beneath, putting up two more large birds, hitherto unnoticed. All were common buzzards, the first a specimen long enough in the tail to raise at first glance a suspicion that it might have been a harrier. Field Guides and other reference books imply, as I suppose they must, that all individuals of a species conform closely to a standard form. Experience in the field teaches otherwise, adding fresh interest to the study of birds, although introducing an element of complication baffling to the beginner.

We were still far enough from the site for the unchallenged presence of the buzzards to be inconclusive. Soon we sat with the nest in view, under the impression that we could also see a sitting bird. But the breeze had dropped; everything danced and shimmered in heat haze. Because so much of the upper valley lay concealed by the lie of the land when watched from the original OP, we had tried to find a better one, farther from the tree, but more comprehensive in its scope. On a cooler day the move might have proved rewarding. Gathering our belongings, we plodded on to the original vantage point, abandoning our ambitions respecting the head of the valley.

We arrived at exactly 1.00, our sight-seeing detour having doubled the time previously taken to walk up from the car. The hen was on duty, but restless, shifting her position every few minutes. At 2.30, the cock called sharp and clear. To our delight, on craning forward to glimpse a stump just concealed in dead ground between us and the tree, we saw him perched upon it, posing as though for the photograph we wished we were equipped to take. He was a beautiful specimen. If it was not the cock encountered in 1972, it was another from the same mould.

The hen left the eggs, flew to her mate, and hovered briefly over him. Merlins are mercurial in their movements. One cannot always say with certainty precisely what was seen half-obscured by flailing wings in two or three seconds, but it appeared to both of us that the merlins touched bills, as courting cage birds may be seen to do, before the hen broke away to dash off down the valley. Dropping silently from the stump, the cock beat fast across the intervening ground to sail up to the tree-top in plain view. Either he failed to realise that he was observed, or had an unusually trusting disposition.

A few minutes before the relief, an incident had been

observed and noted down. Even when a specific target is under scrutiny, the eye should occasionally be allowed to wander. At 2.20, a cloud of starlings flared up from a sugarloaf hill beyond the far side of the valley. The glasses disclosed a dull brown hawk twisting and flashing in pursuit of a quarry too small to be seen at the distance. With the hen merlin on the nest, the probabilities suggested sparrowhawk: but there was for all that something in the behaviour of the bird which spelt merlin. Could there be *two* pairs in such proximity?

The possibility formed the topic of desultory conversation through the half-hour which followed the relief. The afternoon had grown hotter; cuckoos cadenced or babbled, according to sex. A smoky-blue bird sprinted down the valley. With so many cuckoos present and the whereabouts of the cock merlin so certainly established, there seemed little point in training the glasses on it. Cuckoos, in springtime Radnorshire, are commonplace. Happily, my friend thought otherwise. 'Good grief,' he exclaimed, 'it's *another* cock merlin!' And so it was. Even to the naked eye, the bold orange-gold of the breast was visible as the bird banked 100yd away to change direction; and so was the single broad dark band terminating the immaculate blue tail. The issue was as good as settled. If not two pairs, there were certainly two adult cocks on the hills. It seemed unlikely that the second was without a mate. An hour later, after the next relief, the issue was clinched beyond all reasonable doubt.

One hen sat on eggs: another in the topmost spray of the tree, the birds in ostensibly amicable conversation. Mother and adult daughter? Sisters? Or merely friendly neighbours? That, one might never learn, but from enquiries made later in the year elsewhere in merlin country, it was learned that this social visiting is by no means uncommon among them.

The visiting hen was paler than the incumbent, recalling the hen which nested in 1972. Otherwise, she differed not at all, having the bright yellow legs and yellow cere of the full adult. After a few moments, she withdrew to the small thorn next-in-line down the valley. There, she preened, showing off her charms to advantage. Eventually, she opened her wings to the reviving breeze to be carried aloft. Banking at 50ft, she closed them to stoop directly at us. As we ducked, she pulled away; rising like a rocket to level off and rotate slowly on her axis in the small-diameter thermal rising from a patch of bare grass on the sun-warmed slope. Falling from her pitch, she buzzed the horizon behind us; then circled the valley screaming, as fast as her flailing wings could drive her. If exhibitionism is not an attribute of the species, merlins give a remarkably good impression of it. One might be forgiven for imagining that the merlin recognised in well-disposed human beings a possibly appreciative audience.

More probably, we were the target of a bold threat-display, evolved to impress upon all intruders that the small falcon is not a creature to be trifled with.

Our day ended at 5.45. The hen sat without relief from 3.30. As we prepared to leave, buzzards soared in the glowing late afternoon sky at all cardinal points of the compass. Pipits and wheatears flitted from heather clump to heather clump. Never had I seen so many on the moor. Their ignorance of the ecological role many of them were destined to play in the coming weeks was a kindly dispensation of a not invariably kind Mother Nature.

20

The Northern Site Again

Two days later, we went to check the situation on the more northerly site in very different weather conditions. Front after front assailed the valley, bringing inky cloud formations, icy rain, and barrages of lashing hail. Winter was issuing one of his periodic reminders that his withdrawal from the British scene could never be taken for granted. Hot coffee was at a premium; binoculars were tucked into the shelter of their cases more often than they were in use. It was not a day for high expectations, but the perversity of the birds' behaviour went beyond the inhibitions which such weather might be expected to impose.

Throughout the late morning and early afternoon, there were outbursts of merlin clamour at hourly intervals. These were sometimes confused with the whinnying of kestrels, always timed to coincide with rain-showers, so that our spectacles were bespattered and binoculars out of commission. With one exception, little or nothing was witnessed of what were doubtless stirring events. Early on in the day, in an interval between showers, a merlin had called while Super-Kes hung hovering over the far ridge. Slipping from his pitch, he folded wings to stoop. My friend's binoculars, rivetted to him from first to last, established his target to be the hen merlin which fled screaming from his assault. The cock, if present, offered no riposte.

The valley had been inundated by a wave of incoming ring ousels. Several were paired up and had won territories; most were cocks resting before resuming their journey north. Cuckoos called prematurely in June's broken cadence. At intervals, a flight of homing pigeons circled the valley, their appearances monotonously predictable. Super-Kes displayed brilliantly in the lulls between the showers, his mate sitting tight on her eggs.

Not until afternoon had descended into evening did a merlin show to effect. 'Is that a crow?' asked my friend, seeing an approaching bird with something untypical in the wing-beat. Focusing to check, I saw instead the stone-grey cock merlin 20ft below the eccentric but authentic crow, flying on a diverging course. Veering a little, he crossed the valley 50yd below us, rose to display briefly but gracefully over the ridge behind before quitting the scene entirely. Super-Kes, it seemed, had won for himself and his mate exclusive raptorial rights to the valley. At no time during the day was the crows' nest used in 1973 visited by a merlin: on no occasion was the kestrel's arrogant display flight challenged.

I departed with dark thoughts of bird-lime, a pigeon basket, a long rail journey ending in liberation on the Caithness coast. All illegal: all unthinkable after the clutch had been laid. The ways of Nature do not always march in step with the aims of conservationists anxious to help in the propagation of rarities. It is an aspect of matters which has to be accepted with as good a grace as may be grudgingly mustered.

The following week was spent in the north, introducing my friend to Lake District peregrines. Such is the organochlorine devastation among these noble birds in North America that a birdwatcher living in the USA who wishes to watch them is more likely to satisfy his ambitions if he visits Britain for the purpose. The majestic falcons obliged. While we were away, the merlin site was visited by an observer who watched for a day without sight or sound of one. Super-Kes added fresh laurels to his formidable reputation by downing a carrion crow, then bursting away feathers to draw blood visibly in a second assault made while the crow lay spread-eagled on the ground with shock. It was remarkable that Super-Kes should strike and escape unscathed. Eye-witness accounts of serious combats between crow and kestrel usually conclude with a description of a stone-dead kestrel falling from the sky. The hawk may have hooked bill and talons: but the crow wields a dagger-bill with deadly efficiency.

This information having been digested, I decided to devote

14 May to a careful search of the other valleys which seam these hills. In all of them there are hawthorns in which crows have at some time built, and rocks to make attractive perches for falcons. During the winter visits, a number had been marked down for later investigation if necessary.

The search was carried out in much improved weather. The strategy employed was based on the theory that during a three-hour stint a relief – with preliminary conversation – could be almost counted on at any merlins' nest containing eggs. The nesting season of the merlin is more closely circumscribed than that of most bird-species. In Wales, they lay during the few days on either side of 1 May. By the 14th, incubation has reached the stage at which reliefs are regular and likely to be reasonably frequent. So a twelve-hour day could be made to cover three valleys, with time allowed for walking from one to the other.

Thus was the day spent, but without the least hint of a merlin. Buzzards obliged by soaring overhead, irresistible targets for any territory-holding merlin on site-guard while a mate incubated. None suffered interference. Beneath one thorn crowned with a crows' nest lay a cartridge-case, the brass cap still bright and uncorroded. Happily, the small body-feathers lodged in the heather at the foot of the tree were smoky-black, not grey or brown. This evidence suggesting the possibility of active keepering was far from welcome; the gossip of keepers themselves having satisfied me that something less than 50 per cent of the fraternity treat the law protecting raptorial birds with total respect. It may be that the shot had been fired by a sheep farmer. One hoped that he took care to confirm the true identity of the birds brooding eggs in crows' nests before raising the muzzle of his gun.

Finally, all else having failed, the old site was given a last check. Super-Kes sat perched on his favourite rock pinnacle, his mate tight on her eggs. Hatching, if indeed the eggs were fertile, could not be far away.

A pair of crows entered the valley. Super-Kes left his perch, beat up purposefully in the still air with menace sufficient for a peregrine tiercel. The crows, unaware of their peril, landed: one among the boulders, the other in a tree commanding the kestrels' nest. Its sojourn was brief but eventful. Although there was no actual bloodshed, its departure was sped by a kestrel whose every fresh action proclaimed him with renewed emphasis to be a wolf in sheep's clothing.

The forces of natural selection have evolved the kestrel as a species along strange lines. Small rodents and large crawling insects form the basis of its diet, according incongruously with its physical endowment. Sufficiently fast and agile to capture any small or medium-sized passerine, it chooses to hover patiently for vole or beetle in places where small birds abound. Rarely is its attention distracted; such birds as are taken are usually caught in circumstances suggesting that they were mistaken for small rodents half concealed by vegetation. It may be that a special gift for hovering in all climatic conditions (all hawks and falcons can hover to some extent with sufficient help from breeze and thermals) opened to the kestrel, in some ancient era of rodent infestation, an easy way of life: one in which more strenuous skills which it is perfectly well equipped to practise fell largely into disuse. If so, where does Super-Kes fit into the picture?

Is he a throw-back or an evolutionary 'sport'? A kestrel akin to those hunting the hills a million and more years ago, or a mutant through whom new patterns of behaviour might be established for the species? Kestrels of habits conforming to the textbook, prosaic though their way of life may be, outnumber the total populations of all other falcons in Britain many times over. The breadth of their distribution is no less impressive than their numerical strength. Their reproductive output adjusts with sensitivity to the availability of prey. By such criteria is evolutionary success measured. Such kestrels attend to their affairs in an evident spirit of live and let live, tending to avoid conflict with other large birds. Moorland kestrels may now and again mob buzzards, but when one watches them doing so it is difficult to believe that they are motivated by much beyond an urge to play.

When an aptitude for coexistence in tranquillity has been attended by such marked evolutionary success, what benefits are likely to be bestowed on the species by enhanced aggressive instincts? 'He who lives by the sword shall perish by the sword.' Super-Kes may live to sire a race of kestrels whose behaviour will lead eventually to the re-writing of reference books; but I think his career is likelier to end abruptly. Fear, he shows no sign of knowing, nor yet discretion. One day the adversary may be ill-chosen. Some veteran crow, battle-scarred and wise in the ways of hawks, or a raven. Ravens bully eagles. Neither being able to attain a margin of dominance, they and the lordly peregrine share cliff-territories in grudging mutual tolerance. For the raven, the boldest of kestrels is but a negligible entity. There, I think, lies the greatest peril.

As these thoughts passed through my mind, the hen kestrel left the nest to circle the valley. Super-Kes promptly flew to the tree but, to my surprise, made no attempt to incubate. After the eggs had been uncovered for ten minutes, I withdrew, in case my presence had been responsible for the hiatus. One owed something, I supposed, to super-embryos, whatever their successful hatching might mean in the long term to the invaluable merlin population of these fascinating valleys.

21
Return to Radnorshire

On 17 May a fair dawn gave way to thickening weather which persisted all the way from east Worcestershire to the Welsh border. There, unexpectedly, were signs of a clearance. By 11.45 when I arrived on site, cotton-wool cloud floated high in a clear blue sky. Within five minutes, the cock merlin called the hen off the nest from the dead ground up-valley.

During the change-over, the eggs were visible. There were three: two of them deep orange-brown, one paler. As he settled down to brood, the cock positioned them carefully; one under the golden belly which toned so perfectly with the tint of the shells; the others, one under each wing. After thirty minutes, the hen returned. The cock flew to the small tree directly down-valley to preen in full view. Scrutiny was mutual. His toilet complete, he took off to climb high over the valley in wide sweeping circles, making a lightning-fast feint at a passing raven on the way up. Eventually, he levelled off to ride the upper breeze, drifting in and out of the wispy mist-tails of the cloud base.

Towards the far ridge, he canted over and fell, staggering and corkscrewing in his stoop. Whether in pursuit of prey seen moving below or in sheer exhilaration cannot be told; for on flattening out he vanished immediately behind a low ridge concealing a hidden depression in the ground. Half an hour later, he returned, calling the hen off the nest. There was more fiddling with the eggs; and an impression that either he turned them or listened for cheeping, activities previously associated exclusively with maternal solicitude. Again after a thirty-minute interval, the hen returned; silently. A theory began to crystallise, its basis obscured in 1972 by the strange acoustics of the rock-rimmed valley then occupied. The cock dictates the reliefs, ordering his mate off the eggs. The hen takes the initiative in timing her return, but a correlation exists between the length of her periods of incubation and the intervals between. Half-hour stints tend to be followed by half-hour absences, and so on.

This time, the cock left the scene immediately, flying out across the moor, hugging the contours. My watch showed 1.30. It seemed an excellent opportunity to eat my picnic lunch. Five minutes later, as I sat immobilised by a hefty portion of meat-pie in one hand and a crust of bread in the other, a bird was observed approaching fast and low from across the valley, making directly for the tree by which I sat. Cuckoos were as much in evidence as ever. This, presumably, was one of them, behaving with the lack of caution they quite often display in the heat of sexual excitement. The bird swept up into the top of the tree to gaze down at me. A cuckoo regards one with orange-yellow eye set in a meaningless face. As its eyes are positioned on either side of its head, like the eyes of all passerines, it cannot exchange glares with a human observer as this bird did from eyes beautiful and expressive, but fiercely dark. It was an adult cock merlin, calling 'skik . . . skik . . . skik . . .' in a high-pitched resonant tone, a cry I had never heard before. I could have reached him with the tip of a salmon rod.

It was not *the* cock merlin, though. He was a little less blue; and as he turned to spread wings and tail for take-off, there was a hint of intermediate barring on the outer retrices. As he crossed the brook, I finally completed the exchange of nibbled victuals for binoculars. Just in time to see a pale hen flying ahead of him. The resident pair had again been the recipients of socialisation.

At 2.25 the sharp call of a cock merlin rang out from somewhere up towards the head of the valley. The hen moved uneasily, but did not respond. Twenty minutes later, he called again from a nearer perch, with an angry imperative note. This time, the hen obeyed without demur. After several minutes spent in conversation – altercation, perhaps – the cock flew circuitously to the nest, exercising maximum caution and finesse. On settling down, he promptly dropped off to sleep, excusable in the now considerable heat. Two hours later, his spasmodic dozing came to an end. After several minutes of fidgeting, he called with the strange resonant high-pitched note heard from the lunch-time visitor: 'skik skik skik,' but at a faster tempo. Sensing that the sound was almost beyond the frequency range audible to the human ear, speculation was immediately stirred as to the possibility of there being some special purpose or significance to it. Is it, perhaps, a signal pitched to reach the merlin ear at exceptional distances – a form of 'radio communication' between the birds? If so, how may one reconcile its use in the circumstances prevailing earlier in the day? Did the bird call its mate urgently to come and observe the fascinating spectacle of a man eating a meat pie? More likely the note is a distress-signal to be interpreted according to the tempo at which it is uttered. In slow time, in circumstances where a possible hazard has been come upon unexpectedly, it may be a command to the hen not to follow. Given at higher speed by a cock cramped and bored by long incubation, it may have meant 'come quickly'. Evidence in favour of the theory was provided by the arrival of the hen exactly four minutes after the transmission of the signal.

Her stint lasted for an hour and forty minutes, uneventful except for a cock's choice of a branch within a foot of the nest for a preening post. At 6.00 the hen responded promptly to a summons from the dead ground up-valley. A long conversation ensued during which the eggs remained uncovered for five minutes with a carrion crow soaring overhead. As anxiety began to ferment, the cock stilled it by flying in to cover the eggs. Five minutes later, the hen sailed up to the top of the tree, wiped her bill on a twig and took over. It seemed highly probable that at 6.00 her mate had delivered her supper, his eventual covering of the eggs while she fed prompted either by general instinct or by the presence of the crow overhead. After the change-over, there was a full-scale methodical preen, the spread tail conspicuously clear of the least hint of intermediate barring. At 6.40, he left the area. Twenty minutes later, so did I; but in less spectacular fashion.

A week passed before I could visit the merlins again. The day was fine and dry, birds active along the route all the way from home.

The hen was on the nest, the cock on guard in a dead tree down in the valley bottom. Soon, he left; flying fast over the moor, his path a shallow arc leading to the skyline behind. Ten minutes later, I heard a soft call, uttered from near at hand. Edging forward, I found him on the stump between my OP and the tree.

From this he flew to the tree. Following him with the glasses, I saw that the hen had gone; leaving a nest which now contained two eggs and a tiny snow-white nestling. The cock perched on the rim of the nest, craned forward, stroked his first-born of the year from crown to rump with the upper curve of his closed bill, then nibbled gently at the white down. Rarely has a bird given me greater surprise. So much for theories formed earlier that the cock was not allowed near the nestlings until they were within a few days of flying!

He left his perch on the hen's return a minute or two later, but flew back into the top of the tree to watch with evident fascination while she fed the nestling. Just how and when the prey was delivered I cannot say. Usually, it is visible when carried in flight, even when clutched close to the body. But on this occasion neither the cock nor the returning hen appeared to be burdened. Perhaps the feed had been the second made from a kill delivered before my arrival.

Feeding done, the hen again left briefly; the cock remaining on guard. On returning, she settled down to brood. The cock vanished from sight but did not go far. At 11.45, a buzzard which had flown down the valley skimming the heather swept up to hang in the air directly over the tree. A blue missile rocketted up to deal with the situation. The merlin's assaults were pressed home with a little less than the usual *élan*; the buzzard, a large one, met them by rolling on her back with legs extended and talons outstretched to fend off. She departed in possession of her dignity, but did not linger.

The merlin dropped to a new perch well in view, where he sat quietly for twenty minutes. Approaching ravens and crows were watched closely, but none crossed the invisible boundary of the defended area. Black-headed gulls passing right overhead were ignored. Suddenly, the merlin tensed, crouched, launched himself like a stone from a catapult in the direction of the nest-tree. The intruder was a woodpigeon which departed in haste, the merlin almost riding on its back as it sped away down-valley. Whether exception was taken to the pigeon as such, or whether its proximity to the nest struck the sentry as particularly ominous, is difficult to say. Perhaps the general similarity of hue to that of another cock merlin was the factor which released the adrenalin. Whichever, the ferocity of the pursuit ill-matched the innocence of the victim.

There is a fourth possibility. The show put up against the buzzard, responded to with more resistance than usual, had been comparatively ineffective. Did the merlin soothe a bruised ego by using exceptional and unnecessary violence against a bird which could be counted on to flee ignominiously? I think it likely.

On the nest, the hen coordinated preening and brooding with the ready versatility natural to mothers of all young and demanding offspring. Every so often, the nestling emerged from her protecting feathers for a breath of air and a look at the outside world. At 1.20 she left the nest without being called, and flew 100yd down-valley to where the cock stood in the heather mantling prey. A brief but noisy greeting ceremony preceded the transfer of prey which the hen carried straight to the nest, now seen to be occupied by one unhatched egg and *two* fluffy white nestlings. Choice fragments were sliced from the pipit and shared between them. Then more brooding; during which a nestling squirmed out to sit beside its mother, but to be prodded back firmly and unceremoniously after very few minutes.

Half an hour later, the cock returned, calling sharply. The hen's response was a little delayed, but when she flew she left a nest in which there were now *three* nestlings. So far, so good. The hen did not, as expected, return immediately to the nest.

Instead, the cock flew in; to stand straddling the nestlings for several minutes. Presumably, the hen fed on a kill which he had supplied. Matters were complicated at this stage by the arrival of a brown merlin which flew past the nest and away over the moor as though hunting. As will become plain a little later in the story, there were good enough reasons for deciding in retrospect that this bird was not necessarily the resident hen. As though in pursuit of it, the cock departed; leaving the infant nestlings open to the sky and all therein for the four minutes which elapsed before their mother's return. It is the opinion of most field-zoologists that preoccupation with the defence of territory precedes all others. This looked like a case in point.

The next delivery of prey was not until 4.40, signalled by the hen leaving the nest with legs dangling, a sure indication of an intention to alight at no great distance. Three minutes were spent out of view but audible, after which she returned bearing the body of a pipit, stripped as usual of wing and tail quills. The cock followed her; to fly past the tree and away up the valley. Feeding began: a laborious process at this stage because the fragments presented have to be so very small. Before the feed was complete, the cock dropped into the tree, another pipit clutched in his talons. His repeated offers having been ignored by the hen – with an air reminiscent of a young human mother coming upon father offering the new baby a potato crisp – he transferred his prey from talons to bill, taking it and himself off. One sensed that he was playing to the full the role of well-meaning husband injured by the capricious capacity of the universal female to misunderstand the best of masculine good intentions. Perhaps he ate the pipit himself, to comfort his wounded feelings. But if so, he first called the hen repeatedly. He was ignored absolutely. Mother, as usual, knew best.

The cock then flew to the edge of the moor, over towards the fence which marked the boundary between the wild and the cultivated. Here, he landed, to hop and flutter from heather clump to heather clump in an unaccountable way. He may have been trying to flush another pipit (the message regarding the food-capacity of day-old nestlings having failed to sink in) or caterpillars for dessert may have been the object of his search. If nest-robbing was in the repertoire of the merlin, that, too, could have been among the possibilities. But falcons, to the best of my belief, do not indulge in this grisly practice.

Afterwards, he flew to a fence post; where he froze in imitation of a museum-specimen until a deceived pipit fluttered up in display nearby. The merlin, coming dramatically to life, shot up in pursuit to offer the supreme spectacle of a day already rich with incident. The first clutch had missed only narrowly, but the failure proved irretrievable. Five times more, the merlin closed on his quarry, but each time it escaped by a hair's breadth. He then hauled off to climb in spirals, the pipit, too, still ascending. Having at last outclimbed it, he swept in, stooping at a shallow angle on half-furled wings. Again he missed. It was his final attempt. The momentum of the stoop was used for the initial dash at another small bird which had made the error of choosing that moment to flutter up on to one of the fence posts.

Pursuer and pursued vanished into dead ground; I lowered the binoculars. Three minutes later, the cock merlin hovered above the tree calling 'chip – chip – chip', a pipit dangling from his foot by its broken neck. At first, he was ignored by the brooding hen, but when he flew off she followed to collect the booty. Some of it she fed to the nestlings; the remainder she carried somewhere out of sight.

22
Disaster Looms

I seemed fated to precede discoveries of well-positioned merlin sites by making irreversible arrangements to be elsewhere during the first fortnight in the lives of the nestlings. So it was in 1974: the conflicting commitment, a promise to help warden peregrine falcon eyries in the south of Scotland. But this time, I quitted the merlin site with less misgivings than in 1972. The eggs having hatched, egg thieves were no longer to be feared. Before the nestlings reached the stage at which they are at their most attractive to falconers and those fancying a falcon as a pet, I should be back. Casual interference was less of a hazard than in 1972. No track walked by picnickers led to this valley.

Heat approaching Mediterranean intensity made the drive home on 14 June sheer purgatory. The weather experienced in Scotland had been very different. Such a sudden steep rise in temperature often bodes ill. On the morning of 16 June the sky was pregnant with menace. A weird light filtered through dense grey haze, the cloud pall stretching unbroken from east Worcestershire to the Welsh border. The weather forecast had spoken of 'a chance of isolated thunderstorms'. One hoped against hope that the case had not been gravely understated.

As we climbed up the track which led to the moor, the air felt like wet flannel. One sweated and shivered at the same time. Visibility was a little better than might have been expected; oddly enough, a break had formed in the dense grey cloud, allowing a shaft of weak sunlight to illuminate the valley.

During the hour between 1.00 and 2.00pm, two facts were established. The nest contained more than one well-grown well-feathered nestling: both parents were still alive and well. Prey was delivered at 1.15 and 1.50. With light now fading rapidly, it could not be seen whether the feast was shared between two or three nestlings.

At 2.10 the storm broke. First, heavy rain; then plummetting temperatures during which the rain turned to hail. The size of hail-stones is commonly exaggerated by those subjected to their battering. I, too, have in my time spoken loosely of hail-stones 'big as peas'. After this storm had passed, we lay cringing in a bed of hail-stones the largest of which were the size of processed peas after they have been soaked for cooking. They stung the skin through shirt and lined waterproof jacket. They poured down in terrifying density. First, one feared for the lives of the young merlins, helpless in a nest too high in the tree to enjoy much shelter from foliage or branches. Later, one gave up hope for the merlins to fear for one's own fate under the raging heavens. The bombardment by hail was succeeded at last by mere stair-rod rain, but the thunder and lightning mounted to a mighty climax. With the storm centred right over the valley, lightning hissed down time and again to strike the slope opposite, accompanied on the instant by thunder peals to split the ear-drums. One began to see new significance in the remains of long-dead thorn trees standing or lying riven and shattered.

The protection of the car was a good hour's walk away; an hour in which the walker would, on the high bare moorland ridges, function as a mobile lightning conductor. There seemed to be little alternative to lying prone in the heather, suffering in silence.

At 3.30, there came a lull. Binoculars were extracted from sopping wet cases. No sign of life in the nest; the hen a bedraggled ruin perched on a branch of the dead tree in the valley bottom, her saturated feathers plastered to her shrunken body. A fresh bank of ominous cloud loomed up over the horizon: the original storm was unmistakably in the course of circling back, as thunderstorms will.

Our 'waterproofs' were now that in name only, and every stitch of clothing was saturated. Thus attired, we beat our retreat. Gullies usually dry ran a foot deep and more with racing flood water. Between the heather clumps, the moor shone white with a carpet of hail-stones. As we reached the refuge of the car, the storm broke afresh with unabated fury. Never had refuge been more thoroughly appreciated.

Nothing worthwhile had been achieved. Even though the nestlings had been seen to be alive and well at 2.00, they must surely now lie battered to death. Inclemency of weather might be no novelty on the moors chosen by the merlin for its nursery, but conditions such as had just been suffered must be 'freak', even by local standards. The trip home was silent and dispirited.

The worst, however, had to be known. On 18 June the sky still wore an unfriendly expression, but the air felt clean and free from tension. My approach to the site at noon was greeted by the hen merlin flying from one perch to another, both near my intended OP. She, at least, had survived the storms; but her presence in itself was inconclusive. For all I knew to the contrary, a hen merlin bereft of her young might haunt the site of her loss for weeks.

Then, the nest-tree came into view; with a bird perched on a high branch. Without delay, the glasses were used to confirm its identity: a nestling, nearly full-fledged. So one, at least, had survived. At this stage in the progress of a brood, a minor disturbance is unlikely to cause desertion by the parents. Therefore, I decided to relieve my anxiety by closer investigation. Dead fledglings were likely to have been ejected from the nest: if eaten by some carrion-feeder, feathers should remain to tell the tale.

Happily, neither feathers nor bodies were found in the heather surrounding the tree. My search was attended by the anxious mother, who circled the valley screaming in protest, perching briefly in one tree after another. I looked up into the nest-tree through a gap in the branches. Two dark eyes stared back at me intently. By side-stepping five paces, I improved my view. Two young merlins perched shoulder to shoulder, bolt upright and immobile; a third completed a perfectly composed picture by sitting horizontally at their feet. All gazed down upon me notably free from anxiety. By lying down in the heather, I calmed their mother's fears as though by pressing a switch, proved by her prompt return to the dead tree in the valley bottom for a thorough preen.

The high-power glasses could not be focused down sufficiently. Through the low-power pair carried for such eventualities, every detail of the fledglings was discernible, down to the individual scraps of down still adhering to their feathers. Within a few minutes, all inhibitions imposed by my presence had been shed. Wings in which primary quills had still to complete their growth were exercised with vigour, stubby tails were spread wide. In the confined space available, each was fanned and mildly buffeted by the others, but none registered objection. All pecked curiously at each other, but without hostility on the part of pecker or pecked. One tried to dismantle the nest twig by twig, but with little result. Crows are competent architects. Two out of three scrambled to perches in the topmost sprays to exercise wings in greater freedom. As the boughs swayed in the wind, one visualised how the initial flight might come to be made; how the occasional nestling quits the nest prematurely with fatal consequences – as in 1972.

But this tree was a good one, with boughs spaced just nicely to form a safety-net in depth, but also sufficiently open to allow a nestling to clamber back to safety after an unpremeditated descent. As the time I had allowed myself drew to its close, the cock called. The youngsters responded by squeeping and calling 'tuk-tuk', a sound I was delighted to trace to its source at last. It would also have been interesting to discover whether this sound was common parlance between parent and offspring, but it seemed too much to hope that feeding would take place while I sat so near. Hoping to be proved wrong, I lingered for another minute or two. Parents and young continued to exchange calls, but the old birds would not come closer. Without further delay, I retreated to the original OP.

Twelve minutes later, prey was delivered and consumed with good appetite. There were three more presentations during the following two hours, the third of special interest. With the young still at work on the second offering, the hen, perched on the rim of the nest, began to scream loudly. A deafening 'yik-

yikking' broke out close on my left. By crawling cautiously through the heather, I was able to see into dead ground on my left. There, on the low bottom branch of a squat thorn, riven by lightning of long ago, sat the cock merlin; a dead pipit dangling by its nape from his bill. The screams of the hen, who could see me, mounted to a crescendo; the cock, who could not, jumped down to a shattered branch which lay on the ground, the pipit still held in his bill. His call grew yet more strident. Drooping his wings, he spread his tail into a broad fan, canted it right forward – well forward of vertical – in the style of a displaying peacock. This must be the ultimate attraction for the female. Although still screaming with panic, the hen came like a bullet to seize the prey in a blinding flurry of wings. Her return to the nest was no less expeditious.

The cock now saw me for the first time. Staring haughtily, he stretched a wing; lifted a foot to scratch his golden chin. Still watching me, he raised his wings slowly until held vertically over his back, muted mightily, and flew away as slowly as a merlin may without stalling.

Was there ever such arrogance?

This kill the hen broke up and fed piecemeal to the fledglings. The previous two had been dropped in whole for them to tear for themselves. This, perhaps, is how she ensures that none go positively hungry without at the same time discouraging initiative. Ten minutes later, she left for the head of the valley. Fifteen minutes after that, while watching the courtship chase of a pair of cuckoos, I spotted a brown merlin in the top of a big thorn down by the stream. The young displayed no interest in her: as she flew to a nearer perch, I realised that it was the 'other' hen, paying another social call. Eventually, she, too, flew out following the course of the stream towards the head of the valley.

Wing-exercising in the tree top continued, a willow warbler exploring the mayflowers between two of the youngsters, undeterred by the vigorous fanning to which it was subjected or the identity of the fanners. The visiting hen merlin reappeared, ungreeted by the fledglings, to preen in a tree 50yd away. Then clamour on all sides: all three young birds giving tongue; a cock and hen flying in line astern in the valley bottom, hen screaming, cock yikking full-blast. From the foot of the hen a kill, presumably her own, dangled as she carried it. Both birds vanished into a patch of reeds by the stream, the noise undiminished. Three minutes later, the cock departed; the hen emerged to mantle her prey in view, screaming in a thin unfamiliar tone which she kept up until the visitor left. Flying out across the stream towards the opposite ridge, she flushed a pipit which she shot after and was still hunting when both birds disappeared over the skyline.

This intrusion having been dealt with, the resident hen settled to feed seriously. With bulging crop, she dozed in the dead tree for an hour and a half. Digestion complete, she flew down to where she had fed, fluttering from clump to clump as though in search of something. She was. Eventually finding the unconsumed remains of her kill, she carried it to the nest and presented it to her family. As she flew, the cock called from somewhere behind me. As she was in the act of presenting her offering, so he alighted in the tree top bearing a bright cock whinchat which he added to the feast: the first instance witnessed in 1974 of a direct presentation by the cock.

His departing flight took him to a tree some distance on the far side of the stream. From there he flew up-valley, to return five minutes later with another kill which he handed over to his mate for presentation. Ten minutes afterwards, at 6.00, he brought in yet another. Three fledglings: three kills in less than twenty minutes. Despite the failure which I had observed, he seemed able to kill more or less to order at necessity.

Thus concluded a day eventful and satisfying beyond anything which seemed remotely possible when we dragged our shivering wet bodies off the moor but two days previously.

23
Out into the World

The squeeping of juvenile merlins greeted my arrival on 25 June; but the nest was empty.

The valley differed in one important respect from those watched in 1972 and 1973. There were no rocks or boulders whatsoever. From the day I discovered it to be occupied, I had speculated on the influence this fact would have on the behaviour of the newly emerged fledgelings and on their prospects of survival.

Again, the morning had been overcast, the cloud breaking as I walked up to the site. The probability of another wetting for man and bird receded, giving encouragement to at least the former. The hen merlin rose from her guard-post in the top of a thorn-bush to circle the area, screaming wildly. As the intruder, terrifying in his bipedal mobility, subsided into an innocuously static hump her panic was calmed sufficiently for her to resume her post and preen.

More squeeping, inspiring a patient and methodical scrutiny of the many trees and bushes within sight and earshot; but without result. An inspection of the ground itself was then undertaken, calling for even greater method and patience: this time, to be rewarded. There, not 100yd away, across a patch of marshy ground on the slope to my right, sat two of the brood on what appeared at that distance to be an ant-hill. As I watched them, pondering on the fate of Number 3, he fluttered off a heather clump 30yd downhill to *walk* up to his sisters, using his wings only at the last moment to assist him in joining them on their small hillock.

From this I assumed that the nest had been quitted before the birds could fly properly; concluding also that the lack of good rock perches in the valley had proved (and would continue to prove) a handicap restricting the speed of their development. It stood to reason that boulders and rock ledges of various heights must offer both encouragement and opportunity for practice flights. Not only that. More important still, they would offer landings from which more adventurous subsequent flights might be undertaken without the effort entailed in labouring up off the ground.

The speed at which an 'aerodyne' moves through the air governs the degree of lift bestowed by the cloven air passing over its aerofoil surfaces. The force of gravity operating on a bird diving off a rock with wings spread combines with this effect for flying speed to be reached before the bird strikes the ground, even when the ground is but a foot or two below. Once the bird is in motion, instinct ensures that wings are beaten to enhance lift. The young bird rises, involuntarily, perhaps, but thereby finds itself with a choice of high perches on which to make its next landing. Clumsy this may be, but seldom so clumsy that it falls to the ground. Practice, although it may not promptly 'make perfect', soon bestows on the tyro a sufficient standard of competence for it to escape from most of the hazards met at this stage.

The youngsters poked about in the grass on their hummock, scrambling freely over each other as they did so; but when one felt the need of a bowel-evacuation, it was interesting to note how a refinement of instinct led it to back away from the others until its vent was positioned beyond the edge of the tussock. In terms of natural selection, one can see the advantage to birds of a strong sense of hygiene. For functional reasons, feathers must not become clogged – hence the amount of preening which goes on.

For an hour and three quarters, the young merlins remained grounded, the hen maintaining a remote surveillance. Then a family party of crows sailed over. With a single note of warning which froze her brood into instant immobility, the hen flew rapidly to the tree best positioned to be a base for intercepting any attempt at interference. As the crows numbered four, I was relieved at their failure to spot the opportunity for rare mischief offered to them. As they passed out of sight, the hen reacted to a new danger. Following her gaze, I found another family party entering the valley, this time, human: man, woman, boy and girl. Their footsteps were hesitating; a map was checked every few paces. The adults wore binoculars; the general impression given was one of harmlessness. Suddenly, they changed direction; their new course leading them directly to where the young merlins still sat motionless on the ground. The hen took off and circled, screaming. I got to my feet; called, signalled with my thumb-stick. To no avail: steadily, they plodded on. Moving quickly down the hillside, I intercepted them before the young birds had been dispersed. A smile, a raised hat, a quiet explanation and all was well. They watched the circling hen merlin with less interest than I would have expected from self-avowed novice birdwatchers and took the route I had indicated.

Inevitably, while these negotiations were in progress, the cock merlin arrived with prey.

No fool that cock. Not a movement or a sound did he make until the strangers had plodded on another 400yd and I had returned to my OP. Then, and only then, did he fly to where the fledglings could see him and would be excited into calling. My principal fear of the intruders had been that they would panic the young birds, sending them fluttering and scrambling in all directions, dispersed for the time being beyond effective parental protection. I could have saved my concern for a better use. At his father's first call, the young cock leaped into the air and flew to him with the speed of a small ballistic missile. Why he had chosen to labour up the hill on foot when first I had seen him defies comprehension. My anxiety and theorisings on relationships between habitat and education were exploded together.

I relaxed, now able to enjoy the day wholeheartedly . . . or might there still be a problem respecting the two sisters? Still grounded, they had as yet given no evidence of sharing their brother's aeronautical abilities. One might have expected a race for the booty; although, on reflection, it was recalled that competitiveness had not been particularly evident in 1972 or '73 during the first few days the birds were out of the nest. To end all further cogitation on the issue, both took off to fly powerfully to the dead tree in the valley bottom, alighting with something not far removed from elegance. Other touch-downs later in the day failed to live up to this high standard, landings tending to be made *on* a sibling when the evident intention had been to alight beside it.

The day wore on somewhat uneventfully. 'Circuits and bumps', as the RAF used graphically to term them, were the order; singly or collectively. Some provided fresh evidence on the strength and nature of sibling bonds between young merlins. Between the sisters, the bond was strong; but the young cock displayed an independance of spirit not seen before in a merlin of his age. When his sisters flew to join him in a tree or on a tussock, they were tolerated amicably enough, but not once did he take an initiative in seeking their company. More proof of individuality of character in raptorial birds!

At 4.10 in the afternoon, two merlins flew in wing-tip to wing-tip, both pale dull brown above, both equally pallid of breast and belly. One alighted immediately in the small thorn directly down-valley from the nest-tree; the other performed virtuoso aerobatics in the air above it. Had the eye recorded their colour correctly, or was the light playing tricks? No. Two of the juveniles were visible, clearly in view. The third – the cock, as usual – was alone in a tree down by the stream, temporarily hidden by the foliage.

Eventually, the aerobat landed, indicating his sex by his exceptionally small size as much as by his evident urge to dominate the scene. Both birds had the bright yellow legs of the adult: neither showed a trace of visible yellow around the nostrils, which, if present, should have been clear at that distance. The juveniles called to the new arrivals frantically, but were ignored. After ten minutes spent in preening, the two pale brown merlins flew off wing-tip to wing-tip, as they had flown in.

The book regarded as the standard work of reference on British birds is singularly unhelpful on the physical appearance of merlins.

Thus it describes the juvenile male and female alike: 'Like adult female and so far as I can discover, usually indistinguishable, but never so grey, especially on the rump, as some females.' This I believe to be incorrect. Where the adult hen is some shade of dull but positive brown, the juvenile is darker and coloured in a hue not easy to describe. In the brown there is more than a touch of purple and a hint of grey; a number of feathers are edged orange-buff, the same orange-buff with which the purplish-brown tail is barred. Also, the tail is tipped stark white. The underparts are tinted and marked in a way which suggests a compromise between the colours of adult male and female; something not so very different from the colours seen on the breast and belly of its cousin the kestrel.

The book goes on to describe a springtime body-moult when the bird is approaching twelve months of age; stating that it is often incomplete until the autumn, by which time 'males are indistinguishable from adult males: females from adult females'. Nowhere in the stages of development is described one in which both sexes have moulted from juvenile plumage into an intermediate stage in which *both* sexes resemble a pallid hen. If wrong on one point – as it undoubtedly is – the book may be wrong on another; due, perhaps, to too much time spent poring over faded skins in museums and too little time spent watching birds in the field. Could it be that some individual merlins do not moult until approaching *two* years of age, their juvenile plumage fading to the colour described due to an exposure to sunlight twice what is usual? Or is there an intermediate plumage between juvenile and adult, a special 'immature' plumage?

Thus much is known. The moor was occupied by a variety of merlins made up as follows. Two blue adult males. Two adult females, one of orthodox colour (the mother of the brood) a second paler in colour, recalling the 1972 hen. Two, possibly three, pale immature birds identified as such by lack of clear yellow on the cere. Three newly-fledged juveniles. Moreover, the 'mystery birds' seemed to be living in some loose form of social organisation. A 1973 brood, still sibling-bonded? A peer-group randomly assembled as they settled on the moor with older breeding birds? Who can say? Strangest of all was that there should be room for doubt. Merlins have been taken continuously for falconry for at least a thousand years.

After the departure of the visitors, two of the juveniles flew to the hummock where first I had found them that day. One hopped down, vanished behind the heather, and reappeared carrying the connected wings and picked skeleton of a bird larger than the usual pipits and chats. This she tossed about for several minutes before settling down to pick at shreds of flesh still adhering. While she was thus engaged, the cock arrived with a kill. This time, all the young birds flew to him. Flailing wings obscured all detail until one bird emerged from the scrum carrying the prey and taking it out of sight in the heather for consumption. Seizing my opportunity, I strolled across to identify the bird remains by the hummock which was, I found on closer investigation, only an exceptionally large tussock of rank-grass. The virtually clean-picked skeleton was that of a juvenile starling, flesh remaining nowhere but on the tibiae. Pipit feathers, too, littered the ground; suggesting that the tussock was a specially favoured feeding perch. Taking a few samples of plumage and the feet, to confirm identification, I returned to the OP.

Scanning the area, I found one or another of the pale brown 'mystery' merlins perched preening on the nearest grouse butt. From there, it flew to the tree nearest to the tussock, enabling me to confirm identity by a close look at its cere. After repeating its preen, the bird flew to the tussock, seized the starling remains and made off with them towards the stream. A kestrel, until then unobserved, fell like a thunderbolt at the low-flying merlin, mobbing it with evident intent to pirate the prey. Screaming defiance, the merlin accelerated, prey clutched firmly to its belly, making for a tiny dead thorn on the far side of the stream where two of the juveniles now sat like domed plum puddings. But they were plum puddings wired for sound. The third, the young cock, rose from an unseen perch, climbing like a rocket, bouncing with the force of his wing-strokes. At 50ft, he

rolled over with pinions fully furled to stoop fiercely at the
unwary kestrel intent on his victim as it twisted and jinked to
shake him off. The kestrel is not a really large bird itself. As he
closed on his target, the young merlin looked, by comparison,
absurdly small. With tail and flight quills not yet fully
developed, it seemed no larger than a mistlethrush. The kestrel
was struck a blow which sent it tumbling head over heels for
10ft, but feathers were not dislodged. The merlin pressed the
attack; the kestrel dodged adroitly to avoid a second buffet. Not
the least attempt was made to counter-attack, the larger hawk
being pushed to the limits of its considerable agility to avoid the
ferocious persistence of its adversary. The conflict ended with
the kestrel closing wings to dive into the top of the tree by which
I sat, only 9ft away. Oblivious of, or indifferent to, my stolid
presence the kestrel carried out running repairs to badly
disarranged plumage. Greyish head, spotted chestnut mantle,
intermediate barring on a slate-grey tail: a male at least two
years old. For a second time in three years a juvenile merlin
whose life since fledging was to be measured in days only had
got the better of a kestrel whose experience of life on the wing
exceeded his own by one hundredfold. My thoughts turned to
the northern site. The extraordinary qualities of Super-Kes
stood out in sharp relief. What a phenomenal bird he must be
. . . or did his easy victory over the other family of merlins
redound to their discredit? The adult cocks seen in
Radnorshire were all distinctly blue in colour. The other bird
had been the colour of steel or rock. Could it be that blueness in
cock merlins is an index of genetic superiority? It seemed not
unlikely, but a conclusion to be reached without pleasure. To
think in such terms of the cock on the northern site felt like a
betrayal.

Down in the valley bottom there was commotion. Changing
target from my neighbour in the tree, I found the pale merlin
mantling the starling remains, confronting two juveniles which
shrieked their outrage. Possession being nine-tenths of the law,
the intruder bent to feed; picking delicately at the remnants of
tibial muscle. Something else had been learned. Merlins were

not wasteful feeders. The task complete, the pale merlin abandoned the skeleton, heading for the far horizon. One of the juveniles took possession, picking with a mournful air at what – if anything – remained beyond bone and feather.

I felt a little proud of how successfully I had observed and recorded facts which could easily have been confused. The final event of the day shrank the inflating ego back to size. In ten seconds of frantic clamour, merlins uncountable were dashing in all directions. When the dust had settled, the hen merlin was in flight over the moor towards the grouse butts, two juveniles were engaged in a tug of war using a meadow pipit for a rope, the cock sat preening on the topmost spray of a nearby tree, the third youngster squeaked disconsolately somewhere out of sight. As to who had delivered what to whom, or when or how, I had not the faintest idea.

24

The End of the Story

The events of two days remain to be recorded: 30 June and 9
July. 30 June was spent taking a final look at the Radnorshire
site; 9 July on the hills where so much of interest had been seen
in 1973. Artistically, it is satisfying to end a story with a bang.
This one ends more with a whimper. Perhaps all true stories
end thus.

There is little to be said of 30 June without repetition. All
three young merlins were alive and well; fighter tactics were
practised, assaults made on unsuitable prey, some too large
and some unrewardingly small. Kills were delivered and
squabbled over. Showers of rain and a mounted round-up of the
sheep flock on the moor complicated matters. A singularly dim-
witted sheepdog provoked from his master a torrent of
obscenity in English and Welsh at which I blenched: I, whose
youth was instructed by sergeant-majors drawn from The
Brigade of Guards and Cavalry of the Line. The disturbance
could scarcely have been greater: to it they responded merely
by playing 'musical chairs' in the trees. The young merlins
were anchored to the valley by bonds none the less firm for
being invisible.

The pale strangers flew in, enabling me to take a second
opinion on the absence of yellow from the cere. On that day I
was accompanied by one possessing sharper eyes than mine.
Apart from that, I came no nearer to solving the mystery of their
precise identity.

As the day ended, the two sisters roosted securely high in
bushy hawthorns. Their bold brother chose to squat in the
heather; vulnerable, presumably, to any prowling nocturnal
fox. Some Welsh shepherds poison foxes, in flagrant
disobedience to the law. For once, I was not sorry to entertain
the thought. But too deep an emotional involvement with

young hawks one has known from the egg is as forlorn as it is difficult to avoid. Eventually, they must fly from one's care and ken to a fate unknown.

With difficulty I resisted the temptation to return repeatedly to the moor in search of reassurance that the bold young cock had not paid a grim penalty for his injudicious choice of roost. If he did, I may never know. Such is the way of Nature. Or, walking the moor one day next spring, I may find bleached but unmistakable feathers lodged somewhere in the heather. Even then, I shall not know their origin for certain. Men and wild birds can rarely be more than ships which pass in the night.

9 July dawned fine and breezy; and remained so. The northern hills were alive with pipits; many fledglings included among their numbers. No tell-tale heaps of feathers were found. Much of the day was spent on the ridge between two valleys: no hawk of any species flew; no merlin; no hobby; no prowling sparrowhawk; not even a hovering kestrel or soaring buzzard. Crows and ravens provided evidence of excellent thermals by the continual use they made of them. For hawks, there could not have been a better soaring day. We strolled to the rim of the valley. Super-Kes sat perched on his favourite rock pinnacle, hunched in isolation. No mate to be seen; no playful young kestrels. What, I wondered, was implied by that? A blackbird – *the* blackbird, in all probability – fussed as usual in his favourite hawthorn, his survival engineered by an interesting concentration of circumstances. A hobby was discouraged, perhaps, by previous failures from a renewed attempt to nest so far north of its traditional range; the valley was denied to both merlin and sparrowhawk by a kestrel as freakish in character as the summer storms of 1973 thought to have brought disaster to the hobby's brood.

The blackbird fluttered in and out of his bush, cackled in needless alarm, and sang rusty phrases which barely recalled his once-melodious warble. His composure was the greater for his ignorance of the fragility of the chain of circumstance on which his survival had been and would continue to be suspended.

The observations of a single day can never be conclusive; but I left with a feeling deep in my bones that no further visit was necessary.

Driving back along the track which skirts the precipitous flank of the formation, movement above the ridge caught my eye. Braking to a halt, I dismounted. A buzzard soared, dodging and weaving. Three juvenile kestrels fell vertically at him in line astern, like a section of fighters attacking a lumbering bomber. They were no ordinary kestrels. A fortnight later, I received an eye-witness report confirming that Super-Kes and his mate had hatched and reared three nestlings some weeks earlier.

I cannot say that I was surprised by the news.

Afterword

Several years have passed since these chapters were drafted. During this time, one thing above all others has become clear. While the threat posed to the welfare of the merlin by the side-effects of agricultural chemicals has diminished, at least for the time being, another of even graver implications has risen to take its place.

That threat is the conversion of heather moor to forestry, a development which has cost us tens of thousands of acres of open country where they were of the greatest importance to moorland wildlife. Although some other raptorial species have adapted to this, if only during the earlier stages of tree-growth, the merlin has not.

Extensive afforestation of moorland with close-planted trees puts an end to the breeding of merlins in the area. The effect is drastic and quick to make itself felt. The merlin does not adapt in any sense: not even by moving after planting from a lost traditional site to one of the fragments of open heather left unplanted for cosmetic reasons in deference to or in token-acknowledgment of public opinion.

Thus, large areas in the north of England and south of Scotland have lost or are losing their merlins. In 1979, the Royal Society for the Protection of Birds published the opinion that the merlins of Wales and the Marches now represented 25 per cent of the national population. Nor should this be taken to imply that Wales has escaped unscathed during the era of conifer afforestation. Much has been lost and more is under threat. In view of the doubts which exist as to whether conifer afforestation in Britain could be justified commercially without subsidisation in some form, the continuing decline of the merlin outside Wales is all the more to be regretted.

In Wales, there are grounds for hoping that merlins are

actually on the increase now. Since the book was written, other sites have been watched, principally in the heather, west of those described. Much has been seen to amuse and instruct, but the instruction has been chiefly to confirm what had already been learned of and from the tree-nesting branch of the family. Mysteries remain to be solved; much more work on behaviour is needed before the solutions are likely to be found.

As in other ornithological matters, the time has arrived for the ball to be passed from the observant amateur to the professional scientist, who alone is likely to have the time and facilities at his disposal to do the whole of the job as it needs to be done. One awaits with keen interest the results of the first comprehensive investigations.